PRAISE FOR

FURNISHING ETERNITY

A *New York Times Book Review* Editors' Choice

"Tender, witty, and, like the woodworking it describes, painstakingly and subtly wrought. *Furnishing Eternity* continues Giffels's unlikely literary career as the bard of Akron, Ohio. . . . An emotionally satisfying narrative . . . Giffels lovingly but never worshipfully traces the craft of coffin-making, and in so doing lets the essence of himself and his father be revealed through action. Only a very skilled engineer of a writer can transform the fits and starts, the fitted corners and sudden gouges of the assembly process into a kind of page-turning drama."

—*The New York Times Book Review*

"[*Furnishing Eternity*] shows him reconciling with mortality while offering an affirmative account of a father-son relationship. Giffels does well as a voice of the Midwest, but this is for everyone."

—*Library Journal*

"Father and son bond over a lugubrious building project in this sweetly mordant saga of death and carpentry. . . . Giffels treats heavy themes with a light touch and deadpan humor, drawing vivid, affectionate portraits of loved ones in the richly textured setting of Akron, Ohio. The result is an entertaining memoir that moves through gentle absurdism to a poignant meditation on death and what comes before it."

—*Publishers Weekly*

"A memoir about building one's own coffin while your best friend and your mother die of cancer hardly seems a natural for a light and engaging read, but with *Furnishing Eternity*, David Giffels has given us an endearing book that is full of wit and warmth. . . . The project of building the coffin allows Giffels to jump off into ruminations about grief, friendships, and family, as well as amusing details about the death industry and woodworking. All the characters are lovingly drawn with a sensitivity that informs the grief."

—*Providence Journal*

"A lifetime's worth of workbench philosophy in a heartfelt memoir about the connection between a father and son."

—*Kirkus Reviews*

"Giffels mixes unexpected humor into an exploration of middle age and mortality. . . . A moving memoir of grief and recovery."

—*Cleveland Magazine*

"*Furnishing Eternity* chooses to face the hard questions with a spirit of humor and hope, like that Flaming Lips song."

—*The Amazon Book Review*

"A meditation on life, loss, grief, and legacy."

—*Newsday*

"Giffels's writing is poetic and lingers in descriptions but still has a flowing yet casual narrative that engages the reader from page to page."

—*Green Bay Press Gazette*

"*Furnishing Eternity* is a graceful and touching book that skillfully interweaves the coffin-building collaboration with an admiring portrait of Giffels's dad, memories of the author's mother, a teacher and avid reader, and his best pal, John, an artist and avid rock 'n' roll fan."

—*The Canton Repository*

"*Furnishing Eternity* doesn't sentimentalize death nor does it idealize those we've lost in order to keep them close at all costs. Rather, it reminds us how a shared act, even the act of building one's coffin, can reveal the unassuming, even pragmatic ways we choose to show our love."

—*The Devil Strip*

"As father and son embark on the project, Giffels's longtime best friend, John, an artist, is diagnosed with fatal esophageal cancer; his rapid decline imbues *Furnishing Eternity* with elegiac power. . . . The memoir is strongest when it's focused on Giffels and his father in the workshop, tactile and immediate, as Giffels evokes the lush grains of wood, the tools' allure, the 'mealy' spray of sawdust."

—*Minneapolis Star Tribune*

"As you might expect, death and loss are close at hand in this memoir, but so is humor, tenderness, and love."

—New York Public Library blog

"Despite its somber subject matter, *Furnishing Eternity* ultimately becomes a love letter to Giffels's life—to Life with a capital *L*, with all its messy, chaotic, incomprehensible beauty that could never fit into such a small box. After all, this is not really a book about a coffin."

—*Akron Life*

"*Furnishing Eternity* bears witness to the second half of the life cycle: Here the adult son ponders the time he has left with his parents before he enters the role of family elder."

—*The Cleveland Plain Dealer*

"An observant memoir, with shares of both whimsy and grief."

—*Akron Beacon Journal*

"Is it possible to write about the death of your mother, the death of your best friend, the coming death of your father, and the inevitable death of yourself in a context that's both honest and lighthearted? Only if you are David Giffels, and only if you also include some practical information about woodworking. This book is like a Randy Newman song."

—Chuck Klosterman, *New York Times* bestselling author of *But What If We're Wrong?*

"Giffels does the rare emotional work of peering behind the curtain of the father-son relationship and examining it under the press of mortality. He writes with honesty, humor, but above all generosity. We could all learn something from these excellent pages."

—Alexandra Fuller, author of *Quiet Until the Thaw* and *Don't Let's Go to the Dogs Tonight*

"Obituary writers know our job is essentially reassessing life through the lens of death, searching for lessons. Giffels's writing is clever, vivid, hilarious, and touching without ever being maudlin. He writes with the humor, expertise, reflection, and precision of Steve Martin, Jessica Mitford, and Bob Vila sharing a drink at a wake. In the process, he and his family have constructed a story filled with lasting lessons for us all."

—Jim Sheeler, Pulitzer Prize–winning reporter and author of *Final Salute* and *Obit*

ALSO BY DAVID GIFFELS

The Hard Way on Purpose:
Essays and Dispatches from the Rust Belt

All the Way Home: Building a Family in a Falling-Down House

Are We Not Men? We Are Devo!
(cowritten with Jade Dellinger)

Wheels of Fortune: The Story of Rubber in Akron
(cowritten with Steve Love)

FURNISHING ETERNITY

A *Father*, a *Son*, a *Coffin*,
and a *Measure* of *Life*

DAVID GIFFELS

SCRIBNER
New York London Toronto Sydney New Delhi

Scribner
An Imprint of Simon & Schuster, Inc.
1230 Avenue of the Americas
New York, NY 10020

First Scribner trade paperback edition September 2018

SCRIBNER and design are registered trademarks of The Gale Group, Inc., used
under license by Simon & Schuster, Inc., the publisher of this work.

For information about special discounts for bulk purchases, please contact Simon
& Schuster Special Sales at 1-866-506-1949 or business@simonandschuster.com.

The Simon & Schuster Speakers Bureau can bring authors to your live event. For
more information or to book an event, contact the Simon & Schuster Speakers
Bureau at 1-866-248-3049 or visit our website at www.simonspeakers.com.

Interior design by Jill Putorti

Manufactured in the United States of America

10 9 8 7 6 5 4 3 2 1

Library of Congress Cataloging-in-Publication Data is available.

ISBN 978-1-5011-0594-4
ISBN 978-1-5011-0596-8 (pbk)
ISBN 978-1-5011-0597-5 (ebook)

Photo on page 145 by Laurie Emery

The afterword appeared in slightly different form on the Atlantic.com.

For my mother, Donna Mae, and my father, Thomas E.

I am a little world made cunningly
Of elements, and an angelic sprite.

—JOHN DONNE, "HOLY SONNET V"

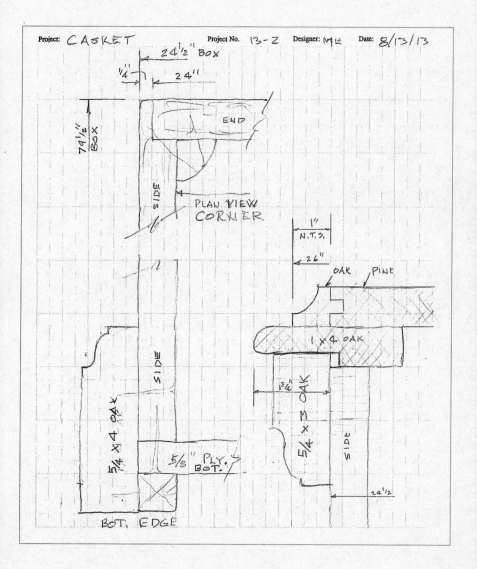

24½" BOX

¼"   24"

79½" BOX

END

SIDE

PLAN VIEW
CORNER

1"
N.T.S.

26"

OAK   PINE

1 X 4 OAK

SIDE

5/4 X 4 OAK

1¾"

5/4 X 3 OAK

SIDE

5/8" PLY.
BOT.

24½"

BOT. EDGE

PART 1

1: THE FAMILY DISEASE

He was sleeping when I arrived, a half-shape through the sun-warmed porch screens, an impression, familiar and calm. It was late spring in Ohio, and the yard surrounding him was dappled with afternoon leaf shadows. A rubbery hum droned from the highway beyond the dense screen of pines and the high stockade fence. Birds chirped. One cloud dragged the sky like Linus's blanket.

He was sleeping. I could see him from the driveway as I slowed to a stop and shifted into park. His old straw hat rose and dipped softly where it rested on his belly. I sat there for a long moment in the beige leather driver's seat, watching through the windshield, engine still running, wondering if I should disturb him.

After a lifetime of driving crap cars, most of which had held the specific purpose of hauling building materials and guitar amplifiers, I had—in what I guess I'll have to concede is middle age—cashed out a very small windfall to buy this seven-year-old Saab turbo convertible. Such a car would seem to imply, if not outright midlife crisis, at least the illusion of leisure. I could have left him alone, put the top down, and gone for a drive in the country.

But I don't go for country drives. Relaxation is not a part of my family's DNA. We spend much of our time trying to outwork each other. My father may have been napping, but it was not a matter of leisure so much as the fact that he was eighty-one years old and had spent the morning chainsawing a fallen tree. So I shut off the engine, pulled out the key, and reached over to the passenger seat for a shaggy folder of notes and sketches, including a couple of drawings from an old *Mother Earth News* article, freshly printed from the Internet: "Learn How to Build a Handmade Casket."

The porch where he slept is a rustic little lodge, cedar post-and-beam, which he built next to the house. It's his favorite place to be when the weather's nice. He spent a year working on it, then another half year fiddling and refining, tweaking the lighting, hanging a porch swing. He still kept the building permit tacked to an inside post, a certificate of ingenuity, of progress, of his own craft. He builds *everything*—he built a bridge across the freaking Rhine River when he was in the Army Corps of Engineers—and the things he didn't build, he changes. He tinkers like it's his job, which, when you're a retired civil engineer, it kind of is. He reads on the porch, Lincoln biographies and good detective novels and every page David McCullough has written. Sometimes when he finishes a book and decides I might like it, he brings it to me. Sometimes I do the same. And he watches the birds here, those yellow and blue flashes outside the screens, looking them up in a thumbed-over field guide he's had for as long as I can remember, and he frets about how to keep the squirrels and raccoons from the suspended feeders, and he often takes his meals here, cooked on the adjacent barbecue under its own pitched roof, which he also built. And he naps here every afternoon, until the changing seasons force him inside.

I approached the porch by way of a ramshackle brick walk, which he'd cobbled from a lifetime collection of street pavers, each stamped with a different name: CLEVELAND BLOCK . . . CANTON BRICK . . . BIG FOUR. Through the screen, I could see him lying on his back across the flowered vinyl cushions of the wicker couch, stockinged feet propped up and crossed at the ankles, hands folded across his chest. He is a man given strongly to quips and mischief; the corners of his lips and eyes have always suggested the hint of a smile. Even here, in sleep, he was grinning about something.

He was dressed in a pair of old jeans and a thread-worn blue T-shirt with a pocket to hold his pencil nubs. He's just under six feet tall, and his hips and legs are narrow, mildly out of proportion with his barrel-chested torso. Arms I remember as muscular are now loose and scaly, yet even when I try to see things as they are, they look the way they used to look. His hair is white, but it doesn't look white by the time it gets from my eyes to my mind. These are among my basic truths—the strength of his arms, the wavy chestnut of his bangs—and the betrayal of time still surprises me. Memory is stronger than fact.

His exposed face and arms bear the chalky scars from countless procedures to burn off skin cancers, a condition his doctors have monitored and treated for years, an ongoing ritual he regards as a necessary nuisance, even as he's had one earlobe and the tip of his nose reconstructed after having them hacked apart to keep the cancer at bay.

He inhaled. He exhaled. The old straw hat with a hole in the crown rose, then sank.

There is an understood circumference around our fathers when they sleep. It's not necessarily a distance of respect. It's first a matter of the smells. Our sleeping fathers are farty, and there's just no way around that. And then there's the pollution of their breath, that stewy vapor of experience, randy and oblique. And more broadly, the resting body's general animal scent, which, like a change in gravity, must be entered carefully.

But ultimately, it's the mystery. A sleeping father is at once mundane and transcendent. Until very recently, the times in my life when I watched my dad sleep were the only times he ever seemed vulnerable. There's something provocative about that, maybe even scandalous. *Him? Something other than invincible?* But now I knew the wider range of his vulnerability. I knew, as he slept, that underneath the thin cloth of that T-shirt was a scar, as healed as it is ever going to be, from the surgery two years before to remove the tumor from his throat. The cancer, he liked to joke, that was not cancer enough to kill him.

That was a rough summer, the only time I've ever seen him scared, and one that prompted a lot of those kinds of jokes, one-liners that I often scribbled on the backs of bank slips and hospital parking receipts and jotted into the pages of the note-book I carried to try to keep track of all the doctor talk. I wrote them down in part because I wondered if these days should be recorded, if they would soon take on a higher and darker impor-tance. Throughout, he was a factory of bons mots and non-answers, thin one-liners that no better hid his discomfort with fear than the hospital gown hid his pale backside.

Small-talk nurse: "So, Mr. Giffels—what did you used to do?"

Dad, slurry and half-loopy from anesthesia: "Chase girls."

Some days, after returning from a session at the Cleveland Clinic, we sat together on that same porch, talking lazily, listen-ing to the way August sounds in this part of the world. It hums a drone note, a delayed, humid countermelody to the heart-swelling rococo of May, the one month that is a true privilege of midwestern citizenship. May in Ohio is a minty, tuneful intoxicant. August in Ohio is a greasy reminder that we have to pay for the good days, sometimes more than their worth. That's just how it is here. August is the time when the sinking reality of being an Indians fan metastasizes into the virgin-soft tissue of the Browns' preseason, that brief period before something is about to go terribly wrong.

So. Through the burn of radiation, he pushed back and pushed back, following doctors' orders but also defying their limits, lifting watering cans and hauling hoses beyond the strict physical restrictions placed upon him. The watering can, he reasoned, got lighter the more he used it. Cancer in the summertime is inconvenient for a country gardener.

Some days, on the half-hour drives to and from the hospital and later, inside the porch, we talked about this project we'd been cooking up, this idea that we would build my coffin. It had come up that same spring, a more or less spontaneous and hypothetical whim that grew into one of those just-might-be-crazy-enough-to-work notions. Not that I was in any immediate need of a coffin, or so I hoped. But, you know, the man was in his eighties, and if I was going to accept his help, it would be best to do it soon.

This was before he got sick.

His long cycle of inhales and exhales continued. I remained near the door, watching him nap. Just beyond the porch, I could hear the chatter of birds at the backyard feeders and, above me, the swish of breeze in a tall, tulipy sort of tree that I wished I could name but, as always, could do so only by asking my dad. Who was asleep.

I returned to the car, set the papers on the seat, and wandered into the yard.

My parents moved to this house in a rural township after downsizing a decade before from the big old house in the city where they'd raised four children. My dad, whose gardens were so elaborate and evolved that, despite their beauty, they were a hindrance in the Realtor's process because of the daunting upkeep, announced that his new life here would be one of low maintenance, inside and out. But we knew that with nearly four acres of land and a retiree's schedule and a life history of extreme restlessness, not to mention the acquisition of a long-yearned-for barn at the rear of the property, he wouldn't take long to renege on his promise. Sure enough, the first spring found him tilling out a kitchen garden and building ornate stone entrance posts, which supported a cedar fence with fat scalloped pickets that he made on his band saw. He fashioned a walkway from scavenged Civil War–era cobblestones. He dug a lily pond. He built a fountain that poured out of a homemade wooden bucket. His determination to slow down was doomed from the start.

On and on it went that way, year after year. He built a bridge across the ravine, laid barn stone for a raised vegetable garden, chainsawed forty-foot trees, hauled the trunks off to be milled into boards, built another bridge across a mostly dry stream (announced by a hand-carved sign reading TROLL BRIDGE, an entirely unnecessary structure that was strictly for the delight of his grandchildren, and himself), built a cuckoo clock from one of the aforementioned boards (cherry), drew up plans for the porch, built the porch, fiddled with the porch so as to prolong its construction, etc.

It's like a battle inside him, maybe a benign one, but fierce and with no foreseeable end. I know this because I've inherited it, and my brothers have, too, and I've called it, not entirely jokingly, "the family disease." A restlessness, a compulsion to keep doing things, doing new things and newer things yet, a discomfort with comfort.

But with a father like that, one whose restlessness and infinite capability carry over into his children's home repair and improvement, there comes an abject and unavoidable fear: How will any of us ever get by without him?

Who will I ask about plumbing flux, about joist loads, about the names of the trees?

In this early June, the grounds were filled with the pinks and whites of newly planted petunias and impatiens and the heady promise of burgeoning cannas and the sort of steady perpetuation that has always been an inspiration for me. Everything everywhere pushing upward and outward, planned and tended and striving for the sun. Plastic buckets by the garage were filled with the bald obscenity of sprouting tubers—elephant ears and calla lilies and yet more cannas, which multiply and multiply, especially in this painstakingly worked earth of his, like teenage lust—the surplus of an acreage too fertile for itself.

And always he was ahead if it, scheming, engineering. In the center of his yard, where it flooded into a swamp every year, he'd planted a bog garden, having researched the trees and plants that would absorb the excess groundwater, and which now thrived in dry soil. Back behind the house, where raccoons had found a way to shimmy up the wide tube of PVC he'd fitted over his birdfeeder pole, he improved on it with an even wider pipe, which kept them at bay, another puzzle solved.

So, yeah, a barn. What better vessel to contain all this, to give it space and shape and scope and possibility?

All my life before this house, I'd known my father's workshop as a staked-out corner of the basement. It was serviceable, although sometimes the table saw needed to be adjusted strategically in order to run a long board through, and the smells of lacquer and the acrid smoke of a dull blade whining through hardwood tended to drift up into the kitchen. The world's mangiest cat slept on the warm insulated steam line overhead, and when it wasn't sleeping, it was swatting glass jars of screws and bolts off the shelves. With the exception of the cat, this was my favorite place as a child, where I sat watching my dad refinish furniture and lay out plumbing repairs and build railings for the porch he added to the back of the house. Sometimes I helped, sometimes I just sat there. Eventually, I started using it myself.

What he really wanted through all those years was a barn. What he had instead was a dinky garden shed that he'd painted country-red and for which he'd fashioned a rustic-looking door with big antique strap hinges, and which he called "The Barn." But it wasn't a barn. It was a shed playing dress-up.

So there was an air of something like coronation and long-awaited arrival when he and my mom moved into this new place, a cozy fifties country house with a big sprawling red barn out back. Inside, he framed a 400-square-foot workshop and spent a season hanging and finishing Sheetrock. He invented and built a brace system so he could raise twelve-foot drywall sheets to the ceiling without a helper. He installed an elaborate dust-collection system and outfitted the shop with heat and water and air-conditioning. Some people retire to Florida, some to the golf course. Midwestern civil engineers dream of settling into a place like this.

And this was why I was here. I'd been waiting for my turn in his workshop. That spring, he was in the finishing stages of building a full bar in my brother's basement, a complex, impressive structure made of salvaged barn timbers, some from my private stash, some from my dad's, and some from my brother's. The men of my family are scavengers of the midwestern sort—we forage and hoard pieces of lumber the way quilters keep soccer jerseys and heirloom kerchiefs. With the bar nearly finished, we'd agreed that this casket thing—whatever it was going to be—would come next.

It had begun as loose talk, speculation over whether the funeral industry even allowed for a homemade casket leading to the reality that it *could* be done. And now here I was, armed with Google research that offered more questions than answers.

The casket still seemed to me, privately, more like a half-baked scheme than an actual project. It worried me some—I have a long history of getting myself into things my pride won't let me back out of. But I didn't reveal this because I didn't want the opportunity to fizzle. I knew that if my dad and I were going to build something so ambitious, we would need to start soon. In truth, what I really wanted was to build *anything* with him, and all the obvious symbolism and cosmic weight of a coffin aside, it wouldn't have mattered if it had been a birdhouse or a Pinewood Derby car or a set of bookshelves. The notion of a coffin had popped up, and I'd clung to it long enough to have arrived here.

What I really wanted was the connection back to that old workshop in the basement, the sweet vinegary smell of sawdust and machine oil. I wanted the old phrenology of dry palm across wood grain. I wanted the yellow extrusion of glue as a steel clamp pulled tight. I wanted the smells of wood stain and urethane. I wanted to support the tail of a long plank as he eyeballed it lengthwise through the table saw. I wanted a reason to be in his dust, brushing it from my jeans and kicking it from my boots and making more.

I returned from an inspection of the front garden, pulled open the porch door, and stood for a moment at the threshold. He awakened the way he has always awakened: suddenly and completely.

"Hey," I said.

"Hey," he said, sitting up and grinning. "I guess I fell asleep."

"Well, I'm here. Ready to do this?"

"Yep."

His bearings regained, he retrieved a woodworker's supply catalog from the floor, then slipped his feet into a pair of rubber garden shoes. We each took a seat at the glass-topped table, and he set the catalog between us. Deep in its pages, at the bottom of a section titled "Project Hardware," was half a page dedicated to casket parts: hinges, latches, handle rod brackets, and an optional "Memorial Tube" time capsule that could be built into the interior.

Along with the catalog, he had a tablet of grid paper, an artifact from his professional days, printed at the top with the name of his company—GBC Design—and blank lines for "Project Name and Number" and "Designer" and "Date." Nearly two decades after retirement, he seemed to have an infinite supply of this paper, and all of us had random sheets of it, each filled with his various plans and drawings for projects. I had one at home titled "Courtyard Entrance" and another titled "Gina's Barn," for a shed I'd never built, theoretically to be named in honor of my wife. (She seemed less flattered than I'd expected.) Each of these drawings corresponded to a pile of building materials I'd salvaged and harbored lovingly.

My father pulled a page from the pad and turned it over to the blank side, then began to sketch with a pencil. His ideas had been forming for weeks. Now he was ready for action.

"I think we should build it out of five-quarter pine, or poplar, number two," he said.

"You mean, like, store-bought?" I said.

"Well, yeah."

My heart sank a little.

"I thought there might be some good stuff in the barn," I said.

I'd hoped to incorporate some of the exotic wood stacked along the back wall of his workshop. He had some pieces of wormy chestnut that I secretly coveted. And I knew there were some cherry planks left from his milled tree. This was partly a connoisseur's instinct for unique lumber, and part selfish desire for recompense—I'd donated some of my very best barn plank-ing to my brother's bar, after all. An atonement was in order.

"There's not enough of any one kind to make it," he said. "We can make it interesting, though. I have some ideas."

With his pencil, he roughed out a pattern showing how we could strap together plain boards with red oak insets, to give the sides some visual texture, kind of like racing stripes. Then he sketched an interwoven L shape to demonstrate how we could join the corners.

"I'd like to do a finger dovetail," he said, drawing a quick model, "but it would be tricky with pieces this big. If we do a butt joint, we can cheat."

"Butt joint," I repeated dryly, emphasizing the "butt."

He smirked. A basic truth: All men, having once been thirteen-year-old boys, will forever after be thirteen-year-old boys. I knew a guy who, in his fifties, broke a hip trying a skateboard move. Instead of accepting this as a cautionary tale, I'd adopted it as a benchmark for my own behavior as my fiftieth year approached.

He continued to sketch his way through the idea, adding a decorative cap to the corner. Then he paused with his pencil against the paper, pulled it away, and looked at what had taken shape there, nodding as though he'd reached a revelation.

"You know what?" he said. "It's just a box."

2 : ROOMS OF OUR OWN

I'd come to this pursuit honestly, which is a nice way of saying it was my father's fault. The house he and my mother raised us in, the house that in many ways made me, was a needy thing, big-boned and drafty, built in the thirties, with a steam boiler in the basement whose humors and balances my dad learned just well enough, which is to say he could maintain it but not tame it. There is some danger in knowing just enough.

Hot iron pipes clanked violently, like baby hurricanes in the walls. All winter, radiators hissed and whistled and bled like hot stigmatas. My mom kept the thermostat high, and the radiator in my brother's and my shared attic bedroom was often searing enough to burn skin. After sledding sometimes, we'd dry our clothes by draping them over the iron monsters, and when they were done, they were rigid and rough and had molded precisely to the shape of the spines. We'd put our sweatshirts back on and fight each other, using the hardened sleeves as clubs.

My father was forever working on that house, repairing and improving, scheming, planning, battling, and lamenting. He enclosed a front porch, creating a room my mother called "The Solarium," the article and caps offering a sort of unearned regality, a room whose sunniness was at tragic odds with its psychedelic shag carpet and its chief resident—a not entirely domesticated green Amazon parrot that screeched like a freeway pileup every morning at dawn. My mother, a lover of words and a devoted crossword puzzler, gave names to everything, each one carefully formulated; language was her version of world order. The parrot was named Mr. Blifil, after the deceitful villain in Henry Fielding's *Tom Jones*. Upstairs, she laid claim to a spare room, which she dubbed "The White Bedroom," and kept the door closed and locked. In shadowy glimpses, I saw piles of shoeboxes and clothing in plastic cleaners' bags, and stacks and stacks of books: *Ragtime; Victory Over Japan; Valley of the Dolls*. Her names covered everything. The basement cat was named Bette Davis Eyes, after the Kim Carnes song, and we had a kitchen island called the Jableebla, for God only knows what reason. Dad made the rooms, and she performed the naming ceremonies. My dad redid the living room top to bottom and gutted the kitchen. Then he blew out a wall to build an ambitious addition onto the back of the house, with a window-filled breakfast room that opened into a two-story porch whose ornate wooden railings he designed and manufactured himself, thick spindles with round decorations in a wave pattern, a style that might be called Victorian Seuss. This spilled outward onto a patio he'd built from repurposed brick and stone, continuing into his sprawling gardens.

It was through his basement workshop that I understood my father best. It was not so much a room as the deliberate staking of a claim. As the White Bedroom was to my mother, the workshop was the room of his own.

The basement was divided into two halves. The first was a rec room, a term needing no further explanation to American survivors of the seventies. Fake wood paneling. Half-assed bar

with a shelf for displaying ceramic steins and novelty cans—
Olde Frothingslosh and Billy Beer. Speckled linoleum floor.
Benches with storage underneath for Risk and Rock 'Em Sock
'Em Robots. Trim painted in that particular shade of "green."

The other half was the real guts of the place: raw old-house
basement with interior decorating by Joe Stalin. Paint-spattered
concrete floor. Pipes cased in asbestos. Metal-framed foldout
windows that didn't work properly and served primarily as inspiration for the glass-block industry. An iron-doored incinerator
built into the wall. Sweaty red-tile foundation. Bette Davis Eyes
lurking in the corners. A stained, bulbous auxiliary refrigerator
idled at the far end, exclusively for Thanksgiving leftovers and
beer. My father bought longneck Blatz by the case.

To my young perspective, this half of the basement seemed
to extend forever. At the far distant end was that beer fridge,
the household laundry operation, and a wall-mounted dial telephone with a black receiver and distressed rubber cord, where
every private conversation was held. Whenever I think of court-
ing Gina as a young college student, I think of sitting atop the
dryer, twirling my fingers through Ma Bell's black coils, trying
to make myself sound interesting.

At the farthest terminus from the laundry was my father's
room, which housed his tools and workbench. It had an old
wooden door made of tongue-and-groove pine, painted white,
with an antique Suffolk latch and a poster of Cheryl Ladd in a
blue satin negligee featuring nine miles of cleavage. My dad was
not the kind of guy who would hang a poster of one of Char-
lie's Angels on his workshop door, but he was the kind of guy
who would receive such a poster as a birthday gag gift, as well as
the kind of guy who threw nothing away. He put the poster in a

place that seemed correct: not hidden, which would imply secret lust, but not exactly public, which would imply ungentlemanliness. He is, above all things, a gentleman.

Cheryl Ladd, then, served as a paper gatekeeper into a room that defined the man as I knew him to be: a highly ordered whimsy. It contained shelves and shelves of labeled cans and jars, nuts and screws and bolts and cotter pins, categorized by size and type; and half-cans of paint lined up like a regiment of spotted knaves, gallons and quarts and pints and spray cans, the dried lapping on their sides offering a rainbow retrospective of rooms and baseboards and fences and chairs; a jelly jar containing three porcupine quills and a bullet shell casing, a preserved legend of his youth; and a large jar of white powder with a handwritten label, "Plaster of Paris," accompanied by a caricature of the Eiffel Tower. Midwestern exotica.

And of course it contained all manner of tools—every imaginable size and configuration of screwdriver (including one that worked sideways!) and saws (including a two-handled crosscut deal that looked like it fell off Paul Bunyan's hay wagon) and hammers upon hammers, but only one true favorite, a black-handled number with a dulled chrome neck and a claw that curved like a shark's fin.

The man owned an actual anvil. Who owns an anvil? Wile E. Coyote, the village blacksmith, and my dad.

I guess this is how I knew my parents—by their effects. I think I understood my mother more through her little crossword table and its accompanying, wild-ranging reference book stack than from any conversation we ever had. My father revealed himself through a generous body of evidence. He became for me a fearless ski jumper, which I knew because I'd seen the trophy, and a man who'd owned a Karmann Ghia convertible, which I knew because I'd seen the photograph, and a man who had dated a Playboy Bunny, which I knew because I'd seen the photo (wow), and who could make smoke come out of his ear and always wore a hat and apparently once shot a porcupine.

I understood my father best when I could enter that space that was uniquely his and, for instance, take up his awl to punch a hole in a piece of leather. I loved to linger there, to find ways to keep myself busy, to sort through his artifacts. In so doing, I began to learn skills allowed by the tools in that room. I could tap out a stripped bolt, solder copper pipe, turn a lathe. I learned the best oil for drilling steel, the best oil for a bicycle chain, the best oil for unfreezing a rusted nut. I used his red draftsman's pencils to mimic the unmistakable script of the engineer: block letters, all caps, straight and square, a penmanship I took up as my own.

When I was ten or so, I established temporary residence in the workshop and built something between a Soap Box Derby racer and the contraptions the Little Rascals were always crashing at the bottoms of hills. It was an elaborate unbalanced thing, a long plank set on axles of my own design, with a rope steering mechanism and a little latched storage space behind the seat. It set my imagination afire, waking me in the wee hours with ideas for improvements and puzzles to solve. I found myself calculating the length of threaded rod I'd need for the axles, figuring the width of the mismatched wheels—which I'd salvaged from a couple of old tricycles—and the washers and bolts. Math I didn't think I knew was coming to me with uncanny clarity.

And so one summer day when I was around twelve, I was exploring the alley behind a short retail strip near my house and came across a stack of discarded plywood sheets, painted ugly green and riddled with staples, chipped and battered, leaning against a Dumpster. They were small enough for me to carry, each one four feet long and a foot wide. That single fact was enough to set my burgeoning machinery into motion. I awoke that night with the moon shining through the attic window and fervently schemed a floor plan whose symmetry fit the perfect math of forty-eight and twelve, the length and width of the boards, the size of *my* boards. I knew the stack of pine studs I could steal from in the basement—my framing. I knew the door that I wanted to use, a heavy antique bathroom door inset with a beveled mirror, leaning against a stack of lumber scraps near the washtub, its surface covered with a wild psychedelia of paint— my dad used it to wipe out his brushes before cleaning them. I had everything I needed. I was ready for a room of my own. I could already hear the ring of my hammer.

The next morning I was back at the Dumpster, knowing the boards would still be there because every boy knows the trash pickup schedules within earshot of his home. I made trip after trip until they were all stacked near the washtub at the opposite end of the basement from my father's room. I worked all day in secret, stopping before my parents got home from work. Within a week, it was done—a slapped-together framework sheathed in green walls, with the doorway carefully measured and framed. Inside, I'd tacked up a board where I planned to mount hooks to hang my few tools. I hadn't hung the door yet because I didn't know exactly how to do that, but I knew my father would know and we could do this part together.

I invited my parents down for the grand unveiling. They saw things quite differently. What they saw is that I'd blocked the path to the laundry, that even my small self had to squeeze between the green plywood and the old lead-covered washtub to get to the washing machine, that a laundry basket couldn't even fit through. They saw that I'd built one wall along the edge of the furnace, blocking access to the pilot light. They saw all the limits of my calculation.

They made me tear it down. I was hurt and bitter. But I was set that day on a path: to build my own version of my father's room.

3 : ARGUMENT

I never wanted a coffin in the first place.

I suppose nobody *wants* a coffin. But I had, for a number of years, built a case against one day being buried in an expensive upholstered Ethan Allen curio cabinet. I developed what passed for an actual position on this matter. I stated my objection with something like passion. Since I came from an old-school Catholic family, the only tradition I knew (and therefore the one I resisted) was the missionary position of American funerals: regiments of bouquets on wire stands, their stink of lavender; address books scrawled with the names of dutiful mourners; Mother Mary prayer cards slid into the pockets of ill-fitting suits. The caskets I'd experienced always seemed so . . . not "me." Too formal. Too shiny. Too old-fogy.

I had determined that these standard mainstream caskets were frumpy symbols of an overpuffed custom that for too long had been allowed to perpetuate without any proper scrutiny, like the first six hours of the Super Bowl pregame or pleats in men's khakis. I'd decided that their style was too JCPenney and not enough Urban Outfitters. I'd decided, apparently, that commercial coffins were *not cool.*

I will admit that I'd never given much thought to the obvious question: What exactly would constitute a "cool" coffin?

All of this obviously says a lot more about my own superficiality than it does about the deficiency of tradition. It also suggests a significant loss of connection with the zeitgeist. In middle age, my style instinct seemed to be on a downhill slide from Coachella to the funeral parlor.

In the Egyptian tradition, the sarcophagus is elaborately decorated with images of the achievements and persona of the deceased, a visual memoir, which seems like exactly the right thing to do but also far too unhumble for the traditional American sentiment. And so we play a constant middle of the postmortem—eulogies that gild and idealize traits like humility and selflessness; insanely expensive newspaper obituaries that read as column-length pathways into paradise. And caskets that are buffed to outshine a Father's Day show car, marketed with hyperbolic model names that sound like political campaign buzzwords—"Heritage," "Legacy," "Defender"—yet at the same time are so generic and devoid of any specific personality that they say nothing at all.

For me, it began right after my father-in-law died. I accompanied Gina, the youngest of his seven children, to the funeral home to help with the arrangements. Her dad, Augustus Owsley Hall (his Kentucky family had a tradition of taking the sons' names from the standing governor, providing he was a Democrat), was a proud World War II navy veteran who attended regular reunions of the crew of the USS *Essex*, an aircraft carrier he called home for four years. For all the satisfactions of his working-class life and the seven children he and his wife of sixty-three years raised, that was his narrative. The *Essex*. So the themes of service and patriotism were at the forefront as we sat together in the sterile, glossed conference room. This particular funeral home had a showroom, with floor models of its casket line displayed with their hoods raised, like Corollas and Tundras at a Toyota dealership. We were ushered in for a tour.

Augustus Owsley was a simple man, a child of the Great Depression, easy to please, and charmingly unfashionable. He wore the same hat every day: a blue USS *Essex* ball cap. When he moved into an assisted care facility near the end of his life and discovered that the cafeteria offered ice cream and beer every afternoon, he knew right then that he would die a happy man. That was all he wanted or needed.

So I couldn't help wondering what he would make of this endeavor. He had no personal style, at least not one that could be channeled directly into one of these wood and steel bed/boxes. He was frugal above all things—his wardrobe consisted almost entirely of yard-sale sweaters and Father's Day gifts. The price tags would be of far greater concern to him than the quality of wood or the gauge of steel. Whenever I heard him asked his opinion of anything, the answer was always, "Just fine." Once, when asked his favorite kind of beer, he responded, "The cheap kind."

As the family listened intently, I eased away from the group. I was curious, though not sure what about. I was looking. For something. And I discovered, at the fringes, a corpse-size cardboard box. My bargain-hunting radar went haywire. *Seventy-five dollars!* And, strangely, it made a statement. It had its own style. The cardboard box, amid all this polish and ostentation, had more presence than any other coffin in the place. It was humble. It was organic. It was rough. It was real. It was muted and impermanent and imperfect and so much more like life. It was a Tom Waits song. It was a relief. It had soul. And it was cheap. *So* cheap.

I moved over to where Gina was grouped with her family. "C'mere," I said, more with facial expression than with words, employing the domestic superpower of marital telepathy.

She casually separated herself from the group and followed.

"There it is," I said. "That's what I want to be buried in."

"You are. Not. Going. To be. Buried. In a *Card. Board. Box.* Absolutely not happening."

Which was the worst thing she could have done. Like many husbands, I am a passive-aggressive contrarian. My strongest convictions are those that animate from an opposing opinion. As soon as I was told that I was not allowed to be buried in a cardboard box, I became absolutely certain that was what I wanted. I knew right then that I would never waver. I spontaneously composed an internal Declaration of Postmortem Independence.

"I am going to be buried in that box right there. You cannot deny me my final wish."

"Your final wish? You're forty-five years old. You're not even sick."

"When I die, I'm going to be buried in that box right there."

"You won't have a say in the matter."

"I've already told you. It's done. You can't just pretend you don't already know exactly what I want. Because I've told you. I want to be buried in a cardboard box. It costs seventy-five dollars."

"Fine. Then I'm just going to put it inside the biggest, most expensive gold vault I can find."

I hesitated. Technically, this meant I had won, and I wondered if it was tactically prudent to protest further.

In truth, her level of conviction was far greater than mine, and generations deep. She is half-Sicilian and had an old-country Grandma Lucia, who, after the death of her husband, threw herself sobbing and shrieking into his casket and wore all black for ten years. So this woman, my wife, has an elaborate, high-concept, hot-blooded Mediterranean approach to the whole *ceremony* of death, and the casket, to her, plays the same role as the rented white limousine in a wedding procession. (Never mind that we departed our church in my dad's leased brown Impala.) I think she found the possibility of hurling her grieving self into a glorified refrigerator carton undignified.

We rejoined the siblings. They had settled in around a gray steel number with a silver crepe interior and long handles suspended from ornate chrome fittings that looked like Dodge Ram hood ornaments. "Sterling," it was called, manufactured by the Zane Casket Company of Zanesville, Ohio. It cost $2,020. The undertaker told us it was eighteen-gauge steel, and I took special note of this, calculating the fact that at the time I was driving a car that hadn't cost much more than $2,020 and wondering if the quality of steel in this vessel was greater than that of my actively rusting Volkswagen out in the parking lot.

Gina's brother, the one who'd taken the lead in these arrangements, pointed out that the gray metal was reminiscent of a battleship, and everyone latched onto this point, so eager for some connection to Dad's legacy. *Of course. It looks like a ship. It's what he would have wanted,* and we nodded as though we'd found our epiphany.

This is the hardest part, isn't it? Making a decision for a parent in the hope not that you have made the "right" choice but, rather, the choice *he* would have thought was the right choice.

The difference between those two is the difference between being someone's child and being your own self—a subtle divide most of us struggle with well beyond the keen of adolescence. What does it mean to be making decisions for the person who first made all your decisions for you, then taught you to make decisions for yourself? What is the sliding scale of "right"? And what if you're wrong?

Also, it was in the lower-middle price range. That helped.

The funeral took place a few days later. As had been the case at my mother-in-law's funeral a year almost to the day before, I was assigned to deliver the eulogy. Everyone else who might have been qualified had declined on grounds that they were afraid of breaking down at the pulpit. Did my appointment indicate their perception of my emotional deficiency? Regardless, I accepted the job and set about the paralyzing task of composing a proper eulogy.

For a writer, the trouble with composing a public tribute is that it eliminates the one thing all writers secretly know is the real truth of the vocation: self-exaltation. We write because it allows us to reveal our hidden awesomeness. The eulogy, however, is the one subgenre that requires perfect humility. You give yourself over not only to honoring the deceased but also to honoring everyone else's memories of the deceased. When the deceased had seven children, seventeen grandchildren, and fourteen great-grandchildren, that's a formula for implosion.

A year before, I'd made the mistake of sending out a group email asking family members to share their memories of Gina's mom. Almost all of them centered on her kitchen table, which felt to me like a windfall—a tangible central image with a shared meaning. A conceit! A motif!

From there, it all went to shit.

"Her pizza," a grandchild wrote. "It was the best."

"Her movie-night popcorn," offered one of the sisters.

"Her cream pie," another grandchild insisted.

"You have to mention her sauce," my brother-in-law wrote.

"Her midnight sandwiches," Gina followed. "I loved her midnight sandwiches. She always shared them with me."

And so on, such that the text began to look more like a Perkins menu than an encomium for the dead. It seemed like the greater the attempt to encapsulate the meaning of a life, the more scattered and ragged that meaning became, even for this simple woman whose legacy was sandwiches and pie.

With the passing of Augustus Owsley, the same issue arose. How to contain the memory of the man? Is it simply a matter of careful arrangement within the logical corners of a box? Does the container have any meaning at all, or does it mock meaning?

Nonetheless, I put on a suit and tie—itself a container entirely foreign to my natural self, but one that Gina will surely dress me in when I die—and I delivered the formal address of remembrance, quilted together from time-softened anecdotes and images, and we adjourned to the cemetery, where the $2,020 eighteen-gauge steel box with silver crepe interior was placed on the rolling mechanism that would lower it into a place where none of this would matter anymore.

Not long before this, I was having drinks with friends at a downtown bar. It was late enough that I had no idea what time it was. A woman approached. She was carrying a small square cardboard box, about the size of a tissue box. She set it on the table as she addressed my friend Bob, who was sitting across from me.

"Hey, do you remember me? I'm so-and-so—so-and-so's friend."

Bob's hesitant expression broke into recognition and he greeted her. "Yeah! How are you?" he said.

"I'm doing great," she said. "We're out barhopping with my daughter. It's her twenty-first birthday. We're celebrating."

She touched the box in a manner that resembled one thing and one thing only—a mother's touch—and the effect was as though the room had just tilted slightly in a way all of us felt simultaneously.

"Well, we're off," she said. "Just wanted to say hello."

She picked up the box and followed her entourage through the room and out the door, off to the next stop.

Bob settled his gaze on me. "That was her daughter," he said, though he didn't need to. "In that box."

For a long time, I lingered only on the oddness of this encounter. But I knew from the moment it happened that the meaning was not mine. Though I could comment, I couldn't judge. A mother had chosen a way to embrace and celebrate her daughter's memory. The daughter, I later learned, had committed suicide in her late teens. I have no doubt that the mother's deliberate method of commemoration is a much richer decision than whether to go with the cherry or the mahogany finish. I think that's when I started to wonder how I might take control over my own final passage.

And if I'm honest: I wouldn't mind if someone took me barhopping in the afterlife.

*   *   *

"I want to be buried in a cardboard box."

"You are not going to be buried in a cardboard box."

Gina and I had been married twenty-five years, over half our lives. Certain words or ideas triggered between us a rich, elaborate shared history, often spinning into well-practiced banter. As with much of the daily (and nightly) interaction of a longtime married couple, just because it's not spontaneous doesn't mean it's not interesting. So whenever the subject of funerals comes up in social conversation, Gina will almost invariably fire up the anecdote machine.

"Oh, don't even get us started on coffins," she'll say, itching for someone to get us started on coffins. "David wants to be buried in a cardboard box. Do you know that a funeral home will sell you one?"

And somehow this topic that would appear to represent a rift between us proves in fact to be something that connects us more strongly. Our argument binds us like opposing magnet poles.

So I'll then move forward, going on about the silliness of Gina caring about the accommodations of the corpse at all, insisting that my body, when I'm finished with it, can be thrown to the coyotes or tossed into the Dumpster behind Hobby Lobby. I toss off these bons mots as though they've just occurred to me, and the only person in the room who knows how road-tested these lines are is Gina, which is to say that only one person truly knows me and my motivations, and she's the one person I'm trying to suggest doesn't understand me. And she understands that I'm doing this, and I understand that she understands that I'm doing this.

That's what half a life together feels like.

I eventually learned that the cardboard box I saw that day was not in fact a legitimate coffin. It was, in the words of the funeral director, a "cremation receptacle," used to transport the body to the crematorium and whose chief attribute, I'm guessing, was that it was flammable or, at the very least, disposable. Upon learning this, I dug around some more and determined that there are very cheap pauper's caskets, under a thousand dollars, often made of low-cost pressboard or high-grade cardboard, and that they are far less expensive than the Sterling, or anything else in its category, allowing me not only to stick to my position but also to back it up with something that sounded like research.

Which is really just proof that my well-crafted, highly evolved protest is evidence that I do indeed give a very large shit about what happens to my body after I die. I just don't know *what* I want done with it. And no one knows this better than Gina.

And so it came to pass: on a March night, we were gathered as a family at the home of my brother's girlfriend to celebrate my dad's seventy-ninth birthday. We were all there: my mom, my dad, their four kids and significant others, their grandchildren. Our family parties are always loud and loose, and as the evening unfolds, they get louder and looser: a game of some sort playing on the big TV, children running pell-mell, adults howling, all of it louder and louder. Depending on location, there might be a dangerous dog involved, or a megaphone, or a parrot screeching with primal urgency. We are, if nothing else, a loud people. It's worth noting the irony that this party, which at least in part acknowledged the remarkable good health of my father as he bore down on his eighties, featured a menu of greasy fried chicken and artery-clogging pizza and free-flowing booze. Life and death, good health and imminent mortality, are always in a state of mingling, like laughing and crying, closer than we might realize.

My father's semi-legendary oldest brother, past ninety, insisted on keeping his driver's license and car after moving to an assisted care facility specifically so he could drive somewhere off-site to smoke cigars all day. This thing that was supposed to kill him was the thing that made his life worth living.

I was sitting across the kitchen counter from my dad as conversation swirled around us. Somehow or other, the subject of funerals came up.

"David says he's going to be buried in a cardboard box," Gina began. "There's no way I'm letting him be buried in a cardboard box." Then, playing a slightly unconventional opening pattern, she preempted the counter-move, jumping right in with: "Did you know you can buy a cardboard casket?"

My dad latched on. "Really? A cardboard box? Can you decorate it?"

I looked at him, and something about his interest set off an old trigger. If there's anything that has connected us over the course of my lifetime, it is the idea of decorated boxes—birdhouses, barns, and most notably, the ramshackle Tudor Revival semi-mansion that he helped me and Gina save from the threshold of condemnation, and which I, for better and for worse, and thanks in great part to him, have been renovating ever since. Gina and I have raised our two children in a drafty twenty-room manifestation of the Family Disease.

My fondest memories of him are of watching him and helping him, learning from him. The last thing I did before moving out of the family home and setting off on my own was to construct an oak file box with finely mitered and fitted corners, built from short planks of A-grade lumber, scraps I'd squirreled away while working as a construction grunt on high-end residential jobs, a box whose antique cup handles I'd selected from one of my dad's fanciful bins of architectural salvage, whose very screws were vintage, collectible, with square brass heads, a box whose finish I'd buffed and rubbed, applying coat after coat, a box whose progress he'd watched and on whose finer points (glue choice, router settings, joinery technique) he'd consulted, a box whose significance was, to me, vital. This box was not just the place where I expected to organize all the writing I was planning on doing in my just-beginning life, but a testament to all I had learned, and evidence that I still needed his help. It was my ritual of departure, my setting-off point, and it returned necessarily to him. As I stood there in that kitchen, leaning on the counter, that box was back home in my attic office, full of ideas and failures and hopeful passages.

"You and I should build my casket," I said.

The corners of the old smile pulled into place. I knew exactly what that meant.

4: AN OLD-ISH SOUL

Although we were born just three months apart, Gina's soul has always been older than mine. As the last of seven children, she was nurtured as much by her siblings as by her parents, who, by the time she came along, were tired and already busy becoming grandparents. She was raised therefore on the glory of seventies AM radio, on Aerosmith and the funk of "Brick House" and Sly and the Family Stone. Her sisters, all married by the age of twenty, gave her wine coolers and hand-me-down bell-bottoms and hard-won lessons about men, work, eye shadow, and the politics of dancing. They lived in tight quarters, in an old house with only one bathroom. The wisdom was hard to avoid.

Her family history is a tapestry of old-country hardship and Appalachian Gothic. She had a Sicilian grandfather who, as a boy, was sold to a chicken farm, where he survived by eating the livestock's feed. He grew up, became a police officer, eventually fled Mussolini, took a ship to America, followed rumors of factory work to Akron, Ohio, and found a job in a tire mill, where he was mocked mercilessly for his accent and his obesity. He lived alone for five years before being reunited with his family, but by then he was a broken man.

Gina had a Cherokee grandmother in Kentucky who, while

still a young mother, committed suicide, leaving her widowed husband to carry on working in a coal mine and raising three boys, eventually migrating to Akron for work in a factory. Late in his life, ninety-some years old, he sat alone with me one Sunday in Gina's parents' living room, mostly blind and deaf, rambling about the time he rented a furnished house and, upon discovering the mattress full of bedbugs, hauled it out to the front yard, doused it with kerosene, and set it ablaze.

"So don't you ever go thinking you're smarter than anyone else," he finished.

Perhaps tellingly, I wasn't sure exactly what he meant by that, but I was certain he knew things I didn't.

From the start, Gina's personal narrative was woven with death and loss in a way that mine was not. I watched her Polish-Russian uncle climb sobbing into the casket of his beloved wife at her calling hours, literally embracing his grief. I'd never seen such a spectacle, yet glancing nervously around the room I realized many there had observed Grandma Lucia perform the same hysteric ritual years before. The night her mother died—the first of either of our parents to pass away—Gina, having witnessed the death, came home so heavily burdened that she crawled on her hands and knees up the stairs. Forty-five years old, she was reduced to a helplessness closer to that of an infant or an ancient. She climbed into the bathtub, a grasp for comfort, and I brought her a glass of wine and handed it to her silently, not knowing what else to do.

I tried to help, and I remember feeling like she suddenly knew a new language I was unable to interpret. Like the foreigner who smiles extra-vigorously to try to convey meaning without words, I became overly solicitous, fumbling for whatever I could offer. Gina's mother, an inveterate bargain hunter, had bought a fancy nightgown on sale at a department store and instructed her daughters that she wanted to be buried in it. For years, we'd stored it for her in a closet at our house. As the funeral approached, Gina's sisters decided together that they wanted to prepare their mother's body for the viewing, to dress her and apply her makeup and set her hair—apparently people do this?—and the undertaker made the arrangements. For Gina, this was a particularly meaningful therapy, as her mother had always come over to our house on Saturdays to have her hair styled in fat rollers while they drank coffee and visited.

In preparation for this grooming, Gina asked me to retrieve and iron the gown, which I did, feeling empowered by the responsibility. On the morning she was to go to the funeral home, I very carefully draped the garment over the passenger seat so it wouldn't wrinkle, only to find my poor wife shocked and rattled by her mother's funeral garb laid out in the unmistakable shape of a body, a ghost riding shotgun.

Still, I tried.

I was aware that the person I knew best in the world had new intelligence that I could understand solely through her. I'd experienced only the losses of grandparents and pets, the training wheels of grief. I was always slow in coming of age, and I always regarded Gina as wiser and deeper in this regard.

When we were dating in college, I would come over to visit at her parents' house after class. Often I would join her in her daily viewing of *Dark Shadows* reruns on the black-and-white portable television in the kitchen. It was her favorite program then, so it was little surprise that her favorite series much later would be *Six Feet Under,* both shows suggesting an appetite for the macabre. With the Cure and Depeche Mode in her record collection, a bookshelf full of Stephen King, a Ouiji board in the closet, and a black pillbox hat with a little veil that she wore sometimes to club shows, accompanied by a long black cigarette holder, she displayed just enough darkness to shade her otherwise sweet demeanor.

She had been interested in my coffin long before I stumbled into the idea of building it, and I have to believe she understood what I was up to better than I did myself.

5: WINGMEN

"Call me."

The text was from my friend John, back home in Ohio. It appeared on Gina's cell phone as she sat across from me at a little sidewalk café in Montauk, Long Island, where we were attending a wedding. She repeated the two words to me, and we looked at each other in the late-morning sunshine, perplexed and a little concerned.

The reason it came to Gina's phone was due to my own stubborn refusal to use a cell phone. I intended to become the last person in America without one. With each passing year, I was certain I could attain this goal. Gina, having grown frustrated with this resistance, had bought me one for Christmas, a slim black Samsung Intensity II "messaging phone." For months I refused to turn it on or learn how to use it. These are the types of goals I set, stubborn matters of self-created principle. (This is the kind of person who resolves to build his own coffin, out of spite.)

This trip to New York was Gina's and my second one that spring, an unusual amount of travel for us, a couple of perpetually broke Ohio homebodies. In March, just before that birthday party of my dad's, we'd spent my forty-seventh birthday in

Greenwich Village, along with John and his girlfriend, Chelsea. Other than Gina, John had been my closest friend since college, and he had always made a particular ritual out of celebrating my birthday, which falls on St. Patrick's Day and therefore is very easy to celebrate in a particularly ritualistic way. Not long before my fortieth, he announced at my kitchen table one evening before we departed for a concert that he was taking me to New York, the city we both loved, to roam around the Village and have lunch at Great Jones Café on the Bowery and window-shop for sneakers in SoHo and see Black 47 play at BB King's in Times Square. He'd already bought the tickets and booked the hotel. When I protested that it was too generous, he responded with characteristic flatness: "Life is short."

John was not particularly expressive, but he was adept with catchphrases and could make even that seemingly empty cliché meaningful. John's life had been dramatic enough for him to have earned the sorts of one-liners usually reserved for B-movie loners and Groucho Marx. We often joked that I could never write his life story because it would come off like bad Loretta Lynn. Years before, for example, in an ultimately futile attempt to save their failing marriage, John and his wife built a dream house in a bucolic village outside Akron. Immediately, it was struck by lightning. When he rushed home from work to address the damage, he spotted his dog on the roadside, dead.

He would recount these stories, cock his head, and intone, "It's a hard-knock life."

In our younger days, we were what might have been called wingmen, though it's a term we would have used only ironically. We were born the same year, graduated from the same high school, became best friends in college, sharing almost every interest. He studied art; I studied writing. We married a year apart, groomsmen for each other. Gina and I bought an old house in Akron, then John and his wife did the same a few streets away. They had a son, then we had a son. They had another son; we had a daughter. We each put down permanent roots in our home-town. John settled into a successful career at Roadway Express, one of Akron's iconic homegrown companies; I found my place at the *Akron Beacon Journal,* the local newspaper.

By middle age, John had become my one friend who still wanted to go to see bands play, who was willing to take road trips to Pittsburgh or Cleveland, who took me to new galler-ies, and who I knew would read the books I loaned him. I kept writing and he kept reading what I wrote, and he kept painting and I kept looking at what he painted. He was divorced and single, with shared custody of his two teenage sons, a corpo-rate job that had him traveling around the world, and a car-nivalesque series of girlfriends. I was married and stable. We struck a good balance: he helped keep me interesting; I helped keep him grounded.

New York never lost its luster for us. Maybe because it rep-resented a kind of shared history; maybe because it represented possibility, something even more precious the longer life goes on. As teenagers in the early eighties, we began exploring under-ground music and culture together, which wasn't easy to access in pre-Internet Akron. On his suitcase-size VCR, John faithfully recorded episodes of *Night Flight* on the USA Network. In his parents' basement, we watched *Eraserhead* and the Clash film *Rude Boy.* It was an education, the pursuit as exciting as the dis-covery. We were acutely aware that New York City was only a day trip away. Manhattan, especially then, was such a different place from our city, dangling the trashy exotica of CBGB's, the Chelsea Hotel, Bleecker Bob's, and Afrika Bambaataa—all within reach. Like Ohio boys since the Jazz Age, we romanticized a New York City that probably doesn't exist, save for the Ohio boys like us who create it.

Our senior year in high school, the spring musical was *My Sister Eileen,* about two artistically minded sisters relocated from Ohio to Greenwich Village, seeking their dreams. It was not lost on me that the play was based on autobiographical vignettes written by Ruth McKenney, who herself had migrated from Akron to New York.

Nor was it lost on John—an avid auteur of jumpy eight-millimeter short films—that much more recently, Jim Jarmusch had left his hometown of Akron for New York and become an underground icon. His film *Stranger Than Paradise*—with key locations on both the Lower East Side of Manhattan and in nearby Cleveland—offered visual, almost mappable, evidence of the juxtaposition that was possible for any of us. It made the romance of New York seem not so very far away. As an art student at the University of Akron, John took a class field trip to the city and returned brimming with excitement and stories, an advance scout of sorts who'd discovered early hip-hop and graffiti and giant slices of pizza with vegetables on top.

The upside of traveling with John was that he took care of everything. The downside of traveling with John was that he took care of everything. It might be unfair to call him a control freak, but he was certainly a control aficionado. If it was a car trip, he drove and knew all the directions and potential detours. If it was a concert, he had preordered the tickets and distributed them as we stood in line. When the dinner check came, he had already slipped his credit card to the server. On our trips to New York, where he visited frequently, he knew in advance which restaurants we would eat at and which museums we would visit. He had made the reservations. He knew where the Joe Strummer mural was in Alphabet City and that he would have me pose there for a birthday photo. He knew where to get Tex-Mex at three in the morning. He knew the best place to watch the St. Patrick's Day parade, which turned out to be on the television in an Irish bar a few blocks away from the actual event, where he could flirt with the red-haired bartender.

For this most recent visit, he'd made arrangements for his frequent-guest discount rate at the Washington Square Hotel; he and the doorman, a charismatic man in a long heavy coat, had a long history together. Knowing that John was coming, the doorman had brought him a gift—a bottle of his homemade hot pepper sauce, which he presented to John as we checked in. John had also obtained four tickets for a St. Patrick's–night Pogues concert at Terminal 5, and had somehow learned about and gained access to a preparty somewhere in Grand Central Station. (Do people go to parties in Grand Central Station? Such things were unknowable to me.) He had plotted the plausibility of getting into Sunday brunch at Prune, a restaurant in the East Village that was the emergent buzz spot for Sunday brunch. The owner, Gabrielle Hamilton, had just released her memoir, *Blood, Bones & Butter,* which would debut that very Sunday on the *New York Times* Best Seller list. There is no logical reason that a middle-aged man from Akron, Ohio, would know that Prune was the place to be on that particular morning, nor that he would know what to say (and I still do not know what it is that he said) to the hostess that got us a table while a sidewalk full of elaborately bearded East Village hipsters idled astride their one-speed bicycles, waiting in vain.

He never did this because he was desperate to be relevant. In fact, he was intentionally invisible most of the time, much more facilitator than agitator. He didn't like attention. It was just this curiosity that he had, a sincere, hungry interest in certain parts of life.

And so we found ourselves in a little bottom-floor corner that Sunday morning at Prune, John and Chelsea and me and Gina. We were served Bloody Marys, and these Bloody Marys were transcendent, they were glorious, they took off the tops of our heads. If Walt Whitman had written Bloody Marys, he would have written these. The swizzle stick was made of beef jerky, with a fat glob of wasabi on the end.

The night before, around one A.M., we'd been walking up Twelfth Street, and just past the Strand bookstore, we were confronted by a moon the likes of which we'd never seen. From behind a drifting cloud, it appeared: a moon as close and bright as an enormous cup of milk. And then, when we got back together the next morning, the first day of spring, and were sipping these Bloody Marys, John, who always knew everything first, informed us that we'd just seen our first supermoon.

Now, three months later, Gina and I were back in New York, at the farthest tip of Long Island, sitting in the sunshine sharing a plate of french fries as the seashore whooshed gently a block away from us. Gina read the text to me. "Why would John want us to call?"

I couldn't answer. I didn't know.

I dialed John's number. It took me to voicemail. "Hey, John. I got your message. We're in New York. Call me back?"

There was no return call.

When we arrived home two days later, another message was waiting. John had cancer. Esophageal. He hadn't told anybody. He'd been in surgery all day, the day after he'd called. They took out his esophagus. His two-word text—"Call me"—had represented a last-minute lapse in his usual stoicism, something I'd seen only a few times before. He hadn't been planning to tell anyone. But then, just for a moment, he'd wanted to allow me in.

Gina and I entered the hospital room that afternoon. John's parents and his brother and sister were there, as well as his two sons and his ex-wife.

With no preparation, I was confronted with a version of my friend I never could have imagined—washed out and bruised-looking, a confusion of tubes and wires, uneasy in half-recline, this man, whom I thought of as a young man, who was my exact age, with whom I had shared so many of life's trivialities and indulgences, never with any consideration of ultimate outcomes, with whom I had specific plans *to drink absinthe*—I had no idea what to say. The words came out on their own: "What the fuck?"

He started to laugh, and all I could do was laugh back.

I was mad at him for keeping this a secret, and confused by his laugh because it was so familiar and unchanged despite everything else. When he laughed, he was himself. As if none of this had happened. We sat for a while, uneasily. Soon everyone decided it was time to let him rest, and when we walked out together, John's ex-wife told me that was the first time he'd smiled since all this began. And in a way that had never been so clear, I knew that he and I needed each other.

So that became the cancer summer. My dad was diagnosed with his throat cancer just a couple of weeks before John. He began a regimen of trips to the Cleveland Clinic, where he'd been fitted for a contraption that looked like Alexandre Dumas's iron mask, a harness that held his head immobile while radiation was fired into his throat. John was undergoing chemotherapy simultaneously. They ran into each other on occasion in the clinic's cancer wing, greeting each other, part of a private club. Some days I drove my dad to his appointment, and sometimes on the highway we talked about this coffin idea, partly as a distraction but also as a way to somehow address the general notion of mortality that was so unavoidable that summer. It was taking on a new meaning, but one that I couldn't fully get my head around.

One afternoon, after returning from the hospital, I sat with my parents in the screened porch, and we got onto the question of the difference between the words "casket" and "coffin."

My mother loved word games. She may in fact be the only civilian in the entire Great Lakes region ever to have owned a complete set of *The Oxford English Dictionary,* an impressive regiment of twenty tall, thick blue spines that covered nearly four feet of shelf space and contained the history of every word in the English language. Because her crossword addiction required a steady supply of reference books, my mother for years had goaded my father to buy her a full set of the OED for her birthday. My dad (correctly) thought this was impractical and extravagant and, at upward of a thousand dollars, unreasonable. But my mother, who was crazy the way everyone's mother is crazy—in her own sweet way—used his resistance as fuel for her utter certainty that she *needed* the OED, she *deserved* the OED, and finally, he, having endured a lifetime of this kind of persistence, relented.

He called me one day and put me on the task of researching where and how one might obtain the comprehensive lexical resource, presuming, I guess, that a degree in English somehow qualified me for the job. I eventually connected with a friend who managed a bookstore, and we ordered a set, which was delivered to my house in several heavy crates.

Not far into this acquisition process, I began to indulge a secret, slightly morbid, yet unavoidable calculation. At some point my mother would die, and this unwieldy set of books would become a family liability. My mother's survivors would be looking for a place to dump it. And I almost certainly would be the obvious beneficiary, and how awesome would I be then, with the complete, unabridged *Oxford English Dictionary* on my shelves. Seriously—there are *libraries* that don't even have a set.

Which I suppose is to say that my mother was crazy in the same way everyone's mother is crazy: in a way that is uncomfortably close to how I am.

casket ('ka:skit, -ae-), Also 6 caskytt, 7 cascate, 9 casqued. [Of uncertain etymology: the form suggests a dim of CASK; but *cas-*

ket in fact occurs earlier than *cask*, and is without precedent as to meaning in Fr. or other lang.

1.a. A small box or chest for jewels, letters, or other things of value, itself often of valuable material and richly ornamented.

When I first looked up that word in Vol. III of the blue-spined books on my parents' shelf, my mother was easing out of her own cancer cycle. After a rough recovery from throat cancer, she had just passed the five-year all-clear designation from her oncologist: the chemo and radiation that had so ravaged her had done its dirty work. Not that she was cured, exactly, but she could proceed with confidence. And so could I and the rest of our family. In some ways, despite the terror and the grind of that experience, her ordeal hadn't triggered the full notion of mortality in me. I'd paid attention to the doctors as I listened in on her consultations, and I'd researched the science as much as possible, and for all the ways that one could—and does—reconcile such hard truths, I'd chosen to settle on this: that she was very lucky to have gotten cancer in the time and place that she did, at the turn of the twenty-first century, with all its advanced treatment, and thirty miles from the Cleveland Clinic, which employs some of the best doctors in the world.

My mother's cancer didn't prompt me to start thinking about death. It prompted me to start thinking more directly about the extension of life. In the midst of her radiation treatments, I quit smoking cold turkey, a ten-year, pack-and-a-half-a-day habit gone. Immediately, I felt healthier, more vital. At the same time, I marveled at my mom's slow but promising recovery.

The experience tricked me into thinking the way a young man thinks: that I had all the time in the world, that possibility is infinite, that I would feel this way forever.

*   *   *

My dad finished his treatments and so did John, and each took remarkable charge of recovery, following all the doctors' orders, eating right, respecting their bodies.

By the Fourth of July, both were well enough to attend a barbecue at our house, though John could only sit quietly in the living room. He was really just there to prove that he could be. He showed me his scar, an ugly purple jag down the front of his now bony torso. He asked me for some books to read. He said he'd been reading a lot about New Orleans. So I ran upstairs and grabbed *A Confederacy of Dunces*, plus Patti Smith's *Just Kids*, a New York book I wanted to share with him, and I returned his copy of *A Moveable Feast*, which he'd loaned me shortly after taking a trip to France with one of his girlfriends.

I'd come to learn that our recent New York weekend was the point when he realized something was wrong. Our morning Bloody Marys and afternoon Camparis and the general over-abundance of food and late nights had been blamed for the relentless heartburn he was suffering. But soon after, John went to see his doctor and learned the truth.

He and I talked quietly in the afternoon shadows of the living room. He couldn't do much. Our friend Kevin had moved in with him for the summer, to take care of the house and help out. He was there, John's attendant, and the three of us made small talk. John told me he'd radically changed his diet. No alcohol. A single cup of coffee a day. He'd tossed out an entire shelf of little hot sauce bottles, a longtime collection of souvenirs from his travels. Even the bottle from the Washington Square Hotel doorman was gone. John was focused and resolute. He would get better.

6: THE CASKET ROOM

I wasn't sure how to dress for the funeral home. I mean, this was a casual visit, and one doesn't generally make casual visits to funeral homes. I was just going there to talk, to ask some questions, to tour the casket room with Paul Hummel, the son of one of my dad's lifelong friends, a fourth-generation funeral director, a guy John and I had gone to the same Catholic high school with, though he was a few years behind us. Casual visit; fact-finding mission. Nonetheless, the idea of wearing jeans to a place that has "parlor" in its nomenclature seemed improper, so I chose gray chinos instead.

Dad and I had roughed out a plan. We had thought about dimensions and hinge configurations and the kinds of wood we might use. For some reason, he kept reverting stubbornly to cedar or white oak, specifically because of their resistance to rot.

"Um, Dad?" I'd say. "What difference does it make if I'm not also resistant to rot?"

He also, for some reason, was fixated on the question of whether the lid should have a lock. He felt that it should. I wondered why.

I had done some research into the practical matters of caskets, a process that had led me to an odd revelation about just how *available* they are. It makes obvious sense. Virtually everyone needs one eventually. Most families have to purchase them on short notice, under terrible duress. But it's not something you think of in terms of the general consumer market.

And yet there they are, all over the Internet. Walmart and Costco and Amazon and Overstock.com sell coffins. So do specialists: Dignified Caskets and Kismet Caskets and Millionaire Casket and Cowboy's Last Ride Casket Company of Early, Texas. One seller, Casketstore.com, offered a range of themed mural designs, the death boxes airbrushed like midlife-crisis muscle cars. On its site, I found a golfer's casket ("Fairway to Heaven"), a NASCAR casket ("Race Is Over"), and a motorcyclist's casket ("The Last Ride"). For the deceased trucker: "The Last Haul." For the outdoorsman: "Gone Fishing."

I even discovered a company called J&D's Foods that pitched a bacon sarcophagus with this description:

> *Is there a better way to show your love of bacon forever than to be buried wrapped in it? We don't think so.*
>
> *This genuine bacon casket is made of 18 Gauge Gasketed Steel with Premium Bacon Exterior/Interior, and includes a Memorial and Record Tube, Adjustable Bed and Mattress and Stationary and Swingbar handles. It also includes a bacon air freshener for when you get that buried-underground, not-so-fresh feeling.*

But for all that, I could find only one instructional book on coffin construction, and its amateurish, rudimentary approach (not to mention the jacket photo of the author costumed like

a Halloween undertaker, in stovepipe hat and black suit) reaf-
firmed just how much I would need my dad's expertise.

He seized the opportunity and had pretty much taken executive ownership of the project. His engineering grid sheet now
was labeled at the top in his block script:

Project: CASKET
Designer: ME

But the more we sketched and planned, the more we realized
how much we didn't know. And when I say "we," I don't mean
mutually. I mean separately, we each had a lack of knowledge.
My contribution to the lack of knowledge was plain ignorance:
I didn't know what I didn't know. His was something more like
wisdom, the Socratic paradox: he knew enough to know that he
did not know enough. So I arrived at Hummel Funeral Home's
chapel near downtown, armed with a list of my dad's questions:

How do you elevate the upper body?
How should the handles be configured?
Is there a standard size?
Does it need to lock?

I had many questions of my own, a growing number of which
were unanswerable matters of philosophy and self-doubt. This
project was beginning to substantiate the single most troublesome truth of my dad's mortality: I flat-out do not know how I
will ever get by without him.

I arrived on a sunny afternoon not long after the first planning visit on my dad's porch. The place was quiet. Funeral homes

are always quiet, I suppose, but they represent nuanced subsets of quietude. There is the somber musical quiet of calling hours, with their measured coffee-breath conversation and featherbed soundtracks. There is the choked quiet of the consultation, a discomforting calm between the twin storms of death and standing in the reception line. And then there is this: the mundane quiet of a workday afternoon, when everyone is either out on the job or here, pushing paper, proofing prayer cards, waiting for the phone to ring.

One of the other funeral directors answered the door and offered me a seat in Paul's office while he went to fetch him. The office seemed purposely humble and decidedly parlor-esque, with out-of-fashion honey-toned wood paneling, an acoustical tile ceiling, and blue carpeting. The padded armchair I sat in was of the type one might find in a great-aunt's living room. I felt remarkably comfortable here. I guessed this was why they called it a funeral "home."

Paul arrived, dressed in a dark blue suit, crisp white shirt, and blue-and-gold-striped necktie. I was glad I'd chosen the chinos. He greeted me cheerfully. He was tall and pleasant, with neatly combed dark hair. He had the demeanor of a ward councilman who has no higher political aspirations, a demeanor of service. Like his father and my own father, Paul bears a mystique of mischief, something hiding in the corners of his eyes, a hair-trigger smile. His profession requires, probably desperately, a humor that's ever present even when not expressed, along with an acute instinct for immediate calibration of tone and mood. Day after day, he has to read an audience spontaneously and know what to say and what not to say. Day after day, he has to represent the nation of death and translate for the new immigrant. He had told me not long before that all he ever thinks about is death, and not in a heavy or depressing way, but simply as a matter of occupation and preoccupation. He had told me about driving with his wife and young daughters on the way to a family vacation, how his wife had begun to quietly cry, and when he asked why, she said she had a sudden dread of a car wreck and, glancing toward the backseat, asked, "Can you put two children in the same casket?" And because he's him, he knew the answer: that the question by necessity cannot be just emotional for him, it's also pragmatic. His father, after a lifetime of this, is one of the warmest and most lighthearted men I know, yet unhardened enough that I'd seen him weep at funerals of close friends.

As we started talking about caskets, Paul told me he'd heard of lots of people wanting to do what my dad and I were embarking on. Even he, an avid woodworker, had given it some thought. "People talk about building it," he said, "but life gets in the way."

In truth, he'd had only one instance in his career when a family had provided a homemade casket, and that was a case of financial desperation. The family couldn't afford to buy a manu- factured coffin, so a few of them had gotten together and quickly hammered pieces of half-inch plywood into a crude box.

"I was really worried it would fall apart," Paul confided.

But from a legal and regulatory standpoint, the homemade box was perfectly acceptable. Before I dove into my recent research, my own sepulchral acumen derived mainly from: 1) attending Catholic and Protestant ceremonies; 2) the deluxe boxed set of HBO's *Six Feet Under*; and 3) the Treasures of Tut- ankhamun tour. So I figured bodies had to be embalmed, housed in some sort of state-sanctioned, decorative, satin-lined casket, and buried in a commercial cemetery. I figured there were a lot of rules. In fact, there are very few. Embalming is not required, Paul told me. And for most cemeteries, the only real restriction on the casket is that it fits inside a vault—the container, usually concrete, that a casket goes into before being lowered into the ground, the purpose of which is mainly to prevent the earth from sinking as body and casket decompose. Paul told me that Catholics have become more and more open to cremation, and his funeral home had recently made a major investment in a crematory. The culture was changing. Only a few years before, the first organic cemetery in Ohio had opened, about forty-five miles from where Paul and I were sitting.

But tradition remained. Paul's family business gets most of its caskets from a furniture maker in Ohio's nearby Amish country. In fact, he told me, I could expect that day to meet the Amish fellow who made the deliveries, as he was on his way in the big transport van and due to arrive any minute.

Paul stood up from behind his desk and invited me to follow him through the hallway and into the casket room. It was about what I'd expected: muted and reverential, well lit, polished, and stark. On the wall were cutaway samples of the casket offerings, one after another in varying tones of polished wood, ocher to cinnamon to coffee bean, their names reading like a sixth-grade social studies quiz:

Adams
Roosevelt
Truman
Madison
Jefferson

Wilson
Taft
Harding
Harrison

The caskets offered by Hummel ranged in price from $1,595 to $8,995. A vault would cost another $1,075 to $10,495. The numbers alone encouraged me. For whatever questions my pursuit might prompt, thrift will never be in doubt. There's no way my coffin will cost anywhere near that range. At most, I figured, the final tally will be in the hundreds, not thousands.

These presidential caskets exuded a uniform regimentation, each of the same basic rectangular shape and size, with similar ornamentation and equipment. Paul went back to his office and returned with a tape measure. We sized up a standard box: 29 inches wide, 84 inches long, 22 inches high. That would be a good template, Paul said, certain to fit inside the vault, the standard dimensions of which offered the only real size restriction. He alerted me to take the handles into account when calculating the width—they'd add a couple inches of clearance to either side. Paul crossed his wrists at his waist to show me how the elbows, in the standard funeral pose, represent the widest point, and to be aware of that when planning the interior space.

This was all useful knowledge. Paul informed me what happens when a very tall person has to fit into a standard casket (bend the knees) and why a plastic pan is standard at the bottom of the box ("Bodies leak," he said). And he answered my dad's question: no, the lid doesn't need a lock. But a simple latch is a good idea, because you don't want the thing flapping open at the wrong time.

As we stood looking over the glossy, ornate samples, I noticed a handsome, more rustic casket on the floor at the other side of the showroom.

"I like that one," I said.

"You'd like the price, too," he said. "Two thousand dollars."

"Really?"

"It's a cremation casket. It's fiberboard. Come take a closer look."

He went over to the box and lowered himself to one knee. He started to open the lid, then suddenly closed it and put his free hand to his mouth. "Ooh—someone's in there!"

Stunned, I shrank back. He looked up at me, paused, then cracked a big grin. I shook my head and thought of a bad word that I shouldn't be thinking in a funeral parlor.

After we were finished in the main casket room, he led me into an adjacent room, where shelves displayed cremation vessels for humans and pets. Hummel's most recent expansion has been into pet cremation, a thriving trend in the mortuary world. Paul told me that one of the most surprising revelations has been that people are far, far more likely to break down emotionally when making arrangements for the burial of a pet than for the burial of a parent.

"Really?" I said. "Why?"

"I think with a parent, they've lived a long life, and if they were ill, they were in the hands of a medical professional. With a pet, it's the owner that made the decision to end the life."

We were finished with the tour, and the Amish casket guy still hadn't arrived. Paul and I lingered for a while in the lobby, catching up on each other's kids and our own lives. We talked about trying to get a lunch date together with our dads, maybe a field day to Amish country, where we could visit the factory. Our time had run long, and Paul decided to check and see if our visitor was close. He made a call on his cell, chatted a few moments, chuckled, and bade his Amish friend farewell.

"You may as well go. He's gonna be a while," he said. "He's at the Apple store."

7: THE POSTULANT

When my mother was a very young woman, barely old enough to make a decision, she made one: she joined a convent. And although she lasted only a few months, barely a season, this fact is an integral part of her personal legend, a parallel to my father having dated a Playboy Bunny, a moment of life experience that doesn't ultimately define anything yet nonetheless becomes a defining part of the puzzle of a person. She stayed long enough to realize it was not the life for her, and when she finally made the request for her release, Mother Superior warned her that if she left, she could never return, which probably came across as more comforting than Her Reverence intended.

My grandmother picked up my mom at the convent, and on the car ride home, she said, low and flat, "I think you made the right decision," and without further comment slipped my mother the jade ring she'd left back home with all the other pretty things she wasn't allowed to wear.

It seems to me that she spent most of her life trying things out. One year she was platinum blond; another year she bought a Vespa scooter. She had a disco phase and a country phase and a Liza Minnelli phase. She always boasted that she "knew herself," but that self was always changing. Whatever it was that defined her moment, it defined her moment completely. Until it didn't anymore.

Although she'd recovered fully from her own cancer treatment by the time my father and John were dealing with theirs, the radiation had left her gouged out and increasingly miserable. She had trouble swallowing and therefore ate next to nothing, subsisting on Ensure and Manhattans sweetened with cherry brandy. She was bony and hunched. She refused most of her doctors' advice, wouldn't take her medications, put it all in God's hands. She was her same affectionate self, but for three years or so she carried a mantle of pain, and when she shared her feelings on the matter, it was more often than not about how she was ready for God to take her.

And so the heart attack that struck her one Thursday night seemed at first like another of her self-definitions, as though she was trying on death for size. She started to recover, then slipped, battling back and forth for three weeks. At one point, lying in her hospital bed, feeling a little better, she simpered and croaked to my brother Ralph, "You know how I said I was ready to die? I'm not."

Which was heartrending to hear, because it implied an agency she no longer possessed. But I'll admire her for it nonetheless, her audacious concoction of fatalism, fickleness, and humor.

Then suddenly, sooner than any of us could have expected, we—her family—were ringed around her hospital bed, watching it happen in slow hungry gasps, death pecking at her. That day seems now like a backward unreeling of night, of washed-out afternoon and blurred morning and back into black night. Nearly a dozen of us—my brothers and my sister, our spouses, our kids, my dad—were packed into an antiseptic space not big enough for any of this. All of us were punch-drunk from having been there most of the night, blurred now in a morning sun cut in slices by the slatted blinds, on the strain of strange anticipation, analyzing each gasp and the long spaces in between, measuring and measuring.

In the middle of this, a knock at the door. A priest.

My mother was no stranger to priests, nor to praying. As with everything else in her life, she did her praying to the extreme. She'd had my father build her a morning kneeler, at which she perched each day with her carefully handled prayer book and one of the hundreds of rosaries she had accumulated. The rosaries were everywhere, a trail of colored and opaque beads and thin metal crosses in stiffened plastic packages—on the kitchen counter, on the living room side table, on the bedroom dresser, in the room where she did her crosswords. Every spectrum of blue, pink, green, cream, ebony, and red. Every patron saint, Ambrose and Patrick and Monica and John Bosco, all the Francises, all the Lost Causes, Our Lady of Every Possible Thing, and of course the ubiquitous Mother Mary, her own patron: Madonna was her given name. They came in mail-order packages and jewelry boxes, ordered from vow-of-poverty missions and the Vatican itself. In fact—to my father's great pride and comfort—the nurse reported checking in on my mother the night before and hearing what would become her last words: a full recitation of the rosary. Eyes closed, she'd incanted the old familiar series of Our Fathers and Hail Marys and the Glory Bes and the Mysteries—joyful, luminous, sorrowful, glorious—before slipping back into this final sleep. And she had been paid a visit the day before by a dear friend of my parents, a retired priest, bighearted and warm, who had come to give her his own final blessing.

"Nice to see you," he'd said.

"Nice to see you," she'd said.

By then, it appeared, though none of us could say for sure, that when she spoke, which was in more and more infrequent flashes of consciousness, she was parroting, not engaging in actual conversation. This could be true, but I choose not to believe it, because in the final exchange I had with her, the last thing I said was "I love you," and she answered with her eyes open and radiant: "I love you."

The priest who'd knocked wavered tentatively in the door-way. He seemed as nervous as he did determined. Like he was selling annuities on commission.

I saw my dad's face. I saw that this was exactly what he wanted, that he seemed almost spirited by the sudden appearance.

"Yes. Please. Come . . ."

He entered.

"Let's pray," the man said earnestly.

Ralph was directly in my line of sight. Catching my big brother's glance in a church-type situation, even one this severe, prompted a momentary impulse to suppress laughter. (When you've shared a childhood bedroom with someone, stifling laughter is a basic bodily function.) I could almost see my mom's scolding eye. We dropped our heads. Then a voice cut us short, gravity returning.

"What is her name?"

My dad, who sat exhausted in a chair at the bedside, answered in a choked voice, "Her name is Donna."

"You're the husband?"

"Yes."

The priest reached for his hand. "Let's say a Hail Mary," he said, and we began in unison.

I was standing at the end of the bed and reached out and held her foot, because it was within reach. Under the rough blanket, it felt bloated and hard. My mom's feet were supposed to be the way they'd always been, the way they always will be to me: calloused and carefree, in a pair of wooden-soled Dr. Scholl's exercise sandals, her toenails painted red. Now they were in acrylic hospital socks with rubber no-slip zags, and despite those socks and the blanket, the foot felt cold to me.

As we stood with our heads bowed, chanting the prayer, the room's thick air was cut suddenly by a loud aggressive double chirp, followed by what sounded like a Casio preset mamba beat. *PLURRP PLURRP . . . chit-chit . . . da-da-da-da—chit . . . PLURRP PLURRP . . . chit-chit—da-da-da-da—chit . . .*

Popple Tone. Verizon, 2011.

My cell phone.

I'd turned it on—for the first time in months—to call my seventeen-year-old son, who was on his way here. It was somewhere . . . in my messenger bag? Ringing. Where? Where was it? Under one of those chairs. Somewhere behind me. A hard hot flush ran through me. I tried to jump backward, had to climb over a chair in the cramped room as everyone paused, raising their heads from the prayer, scowling, confused.

"Turn it *off*," Gina hissed.

"I'm trying!"

I wanted to blame her for buying it for me in the first place, but this wasn't the time. I bent and reached under a chair, fumbling through the front pocket of the floppy canvas bag as the clicky drumbeat continued inside. Finally fishing it out, I punched at the keypad to answer.

"Dad?"

"Evan? We're praying."

"I can't find the room."

I edged for the door, awkwardly waved for everyone to continue, and slipped into the hallway. Our son was at the main entrance and didn't know where to go. I told him the room number, the color of the elevator to take, which way to turn off the hallway. I told him to hurry.

And then I realized that I was, for the moment, free. I was not in that room. I didn't have to go back. Not yet, anyway. Maybe not at all. There was no rule, no protocol, no precedent. I could stay here by the nurses' station, leave everyone else inside with the praying priest, claim that I was waiting for my son. It was late morning, and I was tired and wired. The sun, now fully awake and pouring through the window into the waiting area before me, reannounced a world outside that room. It was morning; it was summer. Summer was my mother in her seventies peroxide phase, when she couldn't go in the swimming pool with us, turning her lament into a singalong: "My hair turns green in—chlor-ine!" Summer was oatmeal packets eaten dry when she was off at her college classes, finishing her teaching degree. It was dusk on the patio, her with her gin martini, as we threw stones into the sky to watch the city bats come harrowing down at us. Summer was the delivered mail, the last Scholastic Book Club order of the year: *Captain Ecology: Pollution Fighter* for me; *To Kill a Mockingbird* for her. Summer was Ohio sweet corn, which she ate with such pleasure that it made our lips move involuntarily in mimicry of hers, a primal sharing.

I lingered. Evan arrived, hurrying down the hall, and then he and I went in together. The group prayer was ending. The clergyman was crying. So was my dad. We said the Gloria Patri together—*as it was in the beginning is now and ever shall be world without end amen*—and then the man in the suit took a step backward, cast us a blessing, and departed. The door closed.

She clenched the next stone in her throat.

In her stubborn, single-minded way—traits she passed directly to me—she continued, and now it was hard to tell if she was staving it off or urging it to come. All her praying and preparing and acceptance and regret clenched itself into the next inhale, which hung there again, the way curls of the sea will freeze in the winter just as they're about to crash, suspended, suspended. Maybe she had willed herself toward this end, and maybe this was some manner of control. She had us all here. Evan had arrived, and now we were complete, the people I know she would have wanted at her side. Maybe she really was prepared, more than I thought. She'd said her rosary. She'd gathered her people.

And then an open space. And then another staggered bead. And then—

It hung, suspended, between us.

If there was a surprise, it was the odd beauty of it, sharing in the death of our center.

A quiet concentration moved each of us to a slight alteration of form, slumping shoulders, dropping heads, useless hands, drifting out of her orbit.

8: SLOW RETURN

I saw him coming across the street, dressed for going out, carrying two brown shopping bags. Even from that distance, even with the still unfamiliar slenderness of his frame, he looked the most complete I'd seen him in a very long time. The most like himself. My dad was sitting with Gina and me in the sunroom of our rambling old house, the doors and French windows open, a warm breeze pushing through the muggy late afternoon. It had been in the nineties at the peak of the day, the funeral hours. We'd changed out of our church clothes, and the family had begun arriving. Trays of food were set out in the kitchen and here, on the round glass table in the sunroom. My dad, exhausted and subdued, was sipping a cold beer from the glass I always served his beer in, an old draft glass from Germany printed with the blue logo: BBK, short for Bayerische Brauerei Kaiserslautern, a beer the Germans call "piss brau."

As he approached the arched door that opened to a front patio, I could see even in his carriage the John I knew so well, the look of him having already handled everything, having predicted and solved problems that hadn't yet occurred. He'd been the first to offer help when the news of my mother's death went out, but not in the usual "If there's anything I can do" manner. Instead, he knew we'd need printed programs for the funeral, and so his questions were not about what he could do but what he was already doing: how many copies did I need, and did I have a good jpeg of her photo, and when did I want to meet at his office to put it all together? I'd shown up on Sunday afternoon with a ream of pale blue paper, and we'd sat in his quirkily cluttered office, walls of corrugated steel, action figures and rubber stamps on the desktop, doing what we'd done so many times before, piecing together a handmade publication. What is a funeral program, after all, but a fanzine for the dead?

I opened the door as he approached. He'd been at the funeral earlier in the day, in a suit, but now he was dressed for going out. John was a connoisseur of sneakers and funky wristwatches, and his orange Pumas were paired carefully with a tangerine Swatch.

"I just stopped to drop some things off," he said. "I'm not staying."

I invited him in. I was glad he was here. He'd always been, for me and Gina both, as close to family as anyone who was not actual family. Early on the morning after our daughter, Lia, was born, when I was back home catching a few hours of sleep, he'd stopped at the hospital to see the baby. He sat holding her as Gina lay there in the exhausted post-delivery tangle of hair and gown ties and ID bands. The nurse stopped in and looked first at Gina, then at him. "Did Dad get some rest last night?"

They both smiled. Neither corrected her. "Yeah. I'm good," John said.

We went through the house to the kitchen. John set the bags on the counter. From one, he pulled a bottle of Jameson. From the other, two bottles of red wine.

"Stay and eat," I said. "There's tons of food here. No one can eat this much ham."

"That's okay. I'm meeting someone."

"A girl?"

"Two, actually."

John had an uncanny talent for choosing women who were entirely wrong for him, and his inherent generosity only exacerbated this weakness. For someone so careful about planning, he was reckless in such matters. A few years before, he had relentlessly pursued a beautiful Egyptian bartender named Amina.

"Last name: Business," he proclaimed. "Amina Business."

It didn't work out. It never did. But it did result in an enduring term in our shared language.

"Okay, so you've got Amina business tonight. But you have to have something," I insisted.

"I'll have a glass of wine. In honor of your mom."

"Really?" I said.

John had not taken a sip of alcohol since his diagnosis over a year before. I opened the bottle, poured him a glass, and poured a glass for myself. We returned to the solarium, where my dad sat.

John raised his glass. "To Donna," he said. "*Salute.*"

He sat with us for a while, then he dissolved through the screen door into the waning light, back into a version of the life we'd known.

My dad mourned mostly in private. I know there was emptiness, he allowed as much, told us that he talked sometimes to the woman who was no longer there. But emptiness is a relative thing in a house she'd filled with a lifetime of accumulation. She'd left him something to do, which was a kind of gift, allowing him to take charge. He began first by emptying closets, sorting through the rosaries, having jewelry appraised, donating formal coats and outdated gowns to the theater department at my kids' school. He worked hard to sort out a complicated life—my mother would make claims that, for instance, she could live off the land, then she would buy an unwieldy stack of books about living the simple life. Projects, though, are how my dad makes meaning and how he moves forward in his life, one all-consuming endeavor feathering into the next and the next, a process that has defined him since I've known him, a perpetual motion.

In the early months of this work, he called to ask if I wanted to take custody of the twenty blue volumes of my mother's *Oxford English Dictionary*. Did I want those books? Hell yes, I wanted those books. I made the trek to his house on a cold, ugly Sunday afternoon in the fall and loaded the heavy volumes into the back of my car, driving them to my office at the University of Akron, where I teach creative writing. Employing the dolly I normally used to move barn stones and heavy furniture, I rolled the books in batches into the elevator and up to the English department, where this collection would qualify me as a bona fide academic badass. (The guy in the next office had only the two-volume abridged version of the OED. And he was a *Shakespearean*!) The top shelf was the only place they'd fit, being oversize, and I had to climb onto a chair and then the desk in order to shelve them.

And then there they stood, lined up like an honor guard, greeting me each day when I went in to teach, a welcome connection.

One afternoon, remembering the conversation from what now seemed like a very long time ago, I climbed onto the desktop and pulled down Vol. III. I looked up the entry and spent some time with it, finding many interesting bits about the word "casket," mainly that the United States is the only country where it's routinely used in place of "coffin," which has a much longer and richer meaning as "the box or chest in which a corpse is enclosed for burial," but which, I think, we Americans avoid because "coffin" seems morbid, too close to a truth we'd prefer to soften.

What I found mostly was that I instinctively wanted to share this information with my mother, that these were facts she would have found interesting. Language and reading were the closest bonds we shared. When I was around twelve, she gave me her copy of J. D. Salinger's *Nine Stories* and explained that she didn't think I was ready for it, and that she didn't even necessarily approve of my reading it (partly, I would soon determine, for its liberal use of low-grade profanity), but that she thought I *should* read it, all of which made me feel very special and also somewhat lost in her mystery. "A Perfect Day for Bananafish" to this day exists like a secret between me and the woman in the White Bedroom. I love the stories from that book perhaps more than any stories I've ever read, but I have never bought my own copy, because the precise value they hold for me can be contained only in the copy that was still on my mother's shelf. It was how I made sense of her.

And so it seemed that in the complicated story of my mother's OED—and my mother herself—the appropriate ending would find them shelved here, in the office where I am defined by the written word. That this is where they belong.

But it isn't. They belong back home, with her.

PART 2

9: MEASURE TWICE; CUT ONCE

I lay on my back on the coarse outdoor carpeting of my father's porch, legs fully extended, feet together, arms bent, crossed wrists resting against my belt buckle.

My dad stood over me with a tape measure.

I squirmed, adjusting my torso until my shoulders felt natural and my elbows felt like they didn't need to extend any farther. This was important. The widest point of a corpse at funeral rest is the elbow-to-elbow span. The maximum width is twenty-five inches. Everything needs to fit, like Russian nesting dolls—body in box, box in vault, vault in hole. But first I needed to feel like I was resting comfortably so that one day my lifeless body could be repositioned to appear as though I were resting comfortably, even though the notion of comfort at that point in one's existence seems impertinent.

I held still. He positioned the end of the tape parallel with the bottoms of my feet and fed it out carefully as he stepped backward alongside me, as though measuring a wall space for a new love seat. At the end, he placed his thumb where the tape coincided with the top of my head. "We'll call it seventy inches, give or take," he said, and penciled the measurement onto his drawing pad.

Then he extended the tape again, measuring from my right elbow. Holding the center point tight against my sternum, he drew his index finger across to my left elbow and eyeballed the measurement. "Hmmm. We can squeeze you in at twenty-three inches."

"Really?" I said. "That's pretty close to the limit. How would an extra-large body ever fit?"

I'm not that big—five-nine, medium build. But months before, when Paul Hummel had measured a standard casket to help me with dimensions, the numbers he gave suggested a space that wouldn't seem to accommodate a body much larger than mine.

"Twenty-three inches," my father repeated. "That's what it says."

I held my position. "Let's do it once more," I said, keeping my neck stiff, continuing to stare upward. "This is definitely a measure twice/cut once situation."

Lying like this—rigid, formal, so unmistakably in the traditional posture of a resting corpse—I couldn't help but feel like Barnabas Collins snoozing in the daytime or Screamin' Jay Hawkins taking the stage. My voice wanted to drop an octave and go, "Gooood eeeev-en-ing . . ." In assuming the death posture on my father's porch floor, I had unwittingly entered the creepiness that everybody pointed out whenever I mentioned I was building my coffin. I could hardly blame them. It felt creepy to me.

An unusual cultural trend has been emerging, particularly in Puerto Rico but increasingly throughout the greater United States, of corpses being displayed in elaborate poses, like life-size dioramas. A *New York Times* article (awesomely titled "Rite of the Sitting Dead") featured a photograph of a deceased boxer in his gloves and silk robe, propped up in a boxing ring, and another of a woman in sunglasses seated at a table, a cigarette perched between the dead fingers of her left hand, with the fingers of the right clutching the stem of a full wineglass. A can of Busch beer and a couple of toy New Orleans Saints helmets rested on the table, with a bottle of Jack Daniel's and a widescreen TV on a shelf behind her.

An executive at a San Juan funeral home that had arranged several of these conceptual viewings explained in the article, "The family literally suffers less, because they see their loved one in a way that would have made them happy—they see them in a way in which they still look alive."

The casket pose, on the other hand, carries only one message.

In the long months following the loss of my mother, I was thinking in an entirely new way about a lot of things, especially death. Losing a parent made the concept of mortality less abstract, more real. The sharpness of the pain also delivered a new kind of clarity about this great mystery, but instead of turning that clarity on myself, I turned it on my father. His mortality became urgent to me; I obsessed about it privately, clenching with worry every time the phone rang, constantly working out his age in my mind, the fact that he was seven years older than my mother, that he was increasingly older than most of the listings in the daily obituary pages, a part of the newspaper I had never read before but began to with greater attention. But for some reason, despite my current posture, I could not envision my own body as a corpse.

Nevertheless, my growing awareness of my father's mortality made my time with him all the more precious and all the more urgent. So I'd begun pressing for us to get this casket project moving forward.

He, on the other hand, made it harder than it might seem. In the wake of my mother's death, his private grief had slowly given way to a greater engagement with his family and the world outside the home they'd shared. He was traipsing off to football games with my brothers, having dinner out with anyone who asked, spending long hours finishing the work on Louis's basement bar. In this resurgence, he began to seem like the most alive person I knew. When our high school alma mater went to the football state championship in November, my two brothers and our dad and I made a road trip to the game, joining a raucous tailgate party that ended with me giving my dad victory piggyback rides through the crowd, spilling beer and high-fiving and laughing so hard it hurt. It was the first time I'd seen him truly happy since summer. In the following weeks, he planned and prepared an ambitious, sprawling post-holiday cocktail party with hors d'oeuvres, dips, grilled chicken, cheeses, and desserts, all of which he prepared himself, the first time that house in the country had ever seen such a thing. He seemed to deliberately confront the fact that he didn't have a single day to waste. He grieved for sure, but he did so a lot better than I did.

This was something like a third act for him. First came his bachelorhood, which he'd enjoyed to its fullest, sailboating and skiing and gallivanting through German beer gardens. Then, after marrying at age thirty, he enjoyed a long and full domestic life with my mother. As her health declined, my mother maintained that she wanted to live long enough to celebrate their fiftieth wedding anniversary, which she did, just two months before she died. And now he was alone and finding his way anew.

What the family started to discern soon after my mother's passing was just how much my dad had been carrying her.

Although his own health had rebounded remarkably after his cancer and he remained social and engaged, my mother no longer traveled well, so he stayed close to her side. My dad was kept from doing so many of the things he loved to do and that they used to do together—going to football and basketball games, dining out, traveling. At one point, my dad came down with a debilitating attack of vertigo, and my mom, who had all but given up driving, had to take him to the emergency room. She parked at the top of a small grassy incline, which they had to descend together, and she was so afraid of falling that she clung to him, even as he had to sidetrack at one point to vomit in the bushes. This pathetic-looking pair finally entered the sliding glass doors in such a state that the attending nurse asked, "Which one of you has the emergency?"

He dealt with her loss by making himself as busy as possible, restlessness remaining his perpetual condition. He continued to empty her prodigiously stacked closets, to sort the rosaries, to leaf through her folders of newspaper and magazine clippings and books upon books upon books, the long comeuppance of her old White Bedroom. He retook control of a life that hadn't been entirely under his control.

So it wasn't hard to get him roped into building a coffin with me. But it was hard to fit myself into his schedule.

When the measurements were done, I pulled myself to my feet and took a seat at the table. Dad got to work with the math, something he is preternaturally good at. He figures in three dimensions in his head as effortlessly as I daydream about sex. If I tell him I need to fill a hole with concrete, he can tell me how many eighty-pound bags of ready-mix I need (with an alternate figure if I prefer sixty-pound bags) before I've even begun to work the puzzle.

"Eighty-three by twenty-seven by twenty-three," he said, already determining how the standard lengths and widths of store-bought one-by planks would fit into these dimensions, including the oak strips that we'd be incorporating into the sides and ends.

It was only a matter of a minute or two before he was dictating a shopping list to me:

Number two pine or poplar . . . eight pieces of one-by-eight
Five red oak one-by-sixes
Sheet of three-quarter-inch plywood

"Do you have time to go now?" he said. "We can take my car."

I hesitated, confronted by the suddenness, a realization that we were moving beyond the conceptual, that something as mundane as getting in the passenger seat of his Ford Edge for a trip to the strip-mall hardware store would seal the fact that we were actually going forward with this.

"Yeah," I said a little hollowly. "Yeah. We could go now."

10: LUMBER: A LOVE STORY

I've always felt a swell of euphoria upon passing through the automatic doors of the big-box hardware store. Say what you will about the depletion of the American soul via mass commerce and suburban homogenization (I say such things all the time), but I just can't help feeling that old thrill of anticipation, of electric uncertainty, of pragmatic discovery, of endless possibility. It may be all tamed and standardized and prefabricated and barcoded, but still, whenever I enter that atmosphere, my genetically coded senses lock onto the faint nearby blood-black scent of iron gas pipe and the sour vanilla of cheap stud pine, primal aura of midwestern resourcefulness.

I didn't care that we were nestled between a Bed Bath & Beyond and an hhgregg. When my dad and I entered Home Depot that day, we were reentering every trip we'd ever taken together to West Hill Hardware, an old helter-skelter mom-and-pop in inner-city Akron, perhaps the most enchanting place I know. Its presence goes to the very beginning of my sense memory. I can remember being too short to see over the counter, standing against my dad's leg as he gabbed with the big, sweet, crusty old guy who owned the place, Paul Tschantz, a white-haired man in an undershirt and stained khaki work pants. I remember staring at the rack containing various diameters of wooden dowels as a cat pawed at my shoelace. West Hill Hardware is as much junk store as home-handyman retailer, and it's the only information source I know, other than my father, to turn to with the important questions of *how*: how to make things, how to fix things, how to understand the ways things work. The wide back porch, the potholed parking lot, and the adjacent jumbled garage are filled with architectural salvage, the stuff that makes scavengers tingle with prickly-heat lust—old claw-foot tubs; boxes of opaque Vitrolite tile; secondhand doors stacked against secondhand doors, dozens of them; oak and yellow pine and industrial steel, with questionable cats meandering in and out. The first definite stirring that I was truly becoming a man was when Gina and I bought our first home and I started going to West Hill Hardware with repair issues of my own. Sometimes, when cash-poor, I would charge my purchase to my dad's account, which he'd had forever, and which was penciled into a worn ledger book pulled from under the counter. Paul Tschantz patiently taught me how to dismantle and repair a heavy old brass lockset I'd pulled from my front door, saving me both the expense and the reduced dignity of a new and inferior fixture. His son Richard, the third generation to work in the business, helped me figure out the complicated configuration of a new gas line based entirely on a sketch I'd made on the back of an ATM receipt. West Hill Hardware is scented like a motherland: machine oil, ancient dust, metal filings, and last week's newspaper. It smells like a church, it sounds like my grandfather, and it looks more like home than anywhere except my actual home. It offers the truest of all comforts: a way to self-reliance.

When Gina and I bought the sprawling, tumbledown old Tudor out from underneath the health department's stack of violations, nothing worked. No usable plumbing, no safe electricity, steam lines spraying hither-and-loo like a scene from a Popeye cartoon. The roof was mossy, rotten, and full of holes, the house invaded by an anarchy of raccoons, squirrels, bats, mice, carpenter ants, feral cats, and a wild wisteria growing unimpeded through the third-floor servants' quarters. One day in the early stages of restoration, a plumbing contractor offered to trade me a rehabbed steam radiator, which I needed, in return for the massive old porcelain tub-style kitchen sink I'd reluctantly—after much protestation with Gina—agreed to replace with a more practical modern sink. He said he could use the sink in a rental unit he was remodeling. Months later, my brother Louis asked for my help. He'd bought a salvage porcelain sink from behind West Hill Hardware that he was going to use as a washtub in his old farmhouse, and he needed assistance lifting it onto a trailer.

The minute I saw it, I knew: he'd just paid fifty bucks for my old sink. Turned out it didn't fit in the rental unit kitchen but was a precise fit in my brother's laundry room. That's about the best explanation I can give for the whole "why" of West Hill Hardware.

My dad thrives on these places because he loves stories, and these places are made of stories. He loves reading stories. He loves hearing stories. He loves telling stories. I've heard him relate certain tales more than once, and I hear in each telling the internal rehearsal, the refinements of foreshadowing, punch lines, bits of dialogue. One of my favorites takes place in a local counterpart to West Hill—Reeves Lumber, a little family-owned lumberyard where my father, having earned insider status, was allowed into the back warehouse whenever he wanted to scavenge odd bits of exotic lumber for whatever wild hair he'd happened onto that particular week.

One Saturday, he was the last customer to leave before the lumberyard closed at noon. The old man at the counter, one of the owners, was planning to stick around and work on some project in the back workshop. My dad departed; the old man locked the front door, retreated into the wide-open back shop, and began setting up his worktable. In the process, he accidentally triggered his nail gun—square into the middle of his left hand. Attached to the workbench, he frantically grasped around him, realizing almost immediately that he was beyond reach of anything that could help in any way, and that he was alone, and that nobody was coming back until Monday morning. As men of a certain era and certain stripe will do, he didn't panic, but instead began making plans for a very long weekend spiked to a workbench. He adjusted himself as comfortably as a man can get in such a situation and wished he'd eaten breakfast.

Soon he heard a sound. The front door. Shuffle of feet. His partner had forgotten something and returned. The old man called out, and just like that he was saved, but not before establishing prime stock in the store-counter legend. This story was told countless times—who knows how close it is to the original facts, and who cares?—and it grew in legend all the way up until the night the place burned down, a few years later, in a shocking terminal of black flames.

So our entry now into the brightly lit order of orange steel shelves was not as far removed as it may seem from the wild frontier of those sawdusty backroom lumber stacks.

My dad walks fast, and he doesn't look back. He's always been this way, but as he's entered his ninth decade, it has become a defining feature. Whenever a car full of family arrives at a restaurant parking lot, for instance, he's halfway to the front door before anyone else is out of the car seat. This has earned him a new nickname: "There goes Antsy Pants," we'll say as we watch the back of his jacket disappear into the horizon.

Watching him grow smaller down the high-shelved aisle, I grabbed a battered steel cart from the holding pen and hurried to catch up.

We slowed when we reached the lumber aisle. The selection ritual was about to begin.

The last time I'd bought new lumber was to replace rotting boards on the face of the garage, an entirely practical and unromantic transaction. The last time I'd bought new lumber for a project based on whimsy—which is how I was defining this casket endeavor—was when I stumbled across a slab of salvaged marble that appeared to be exactly the dimensions of a suddenly imagined bathroom shelf unit to cover a radiator. My dad, naturally, dropped over for a visit just as I was beginning and spontaneously designed it for me, drawing up a set of plans on a legal pad with a series of details that never would have occurred to me.

Before moving into a house that sucked all this kind of energy into its repair and upkeep, I'd been following my dad's path, building more and more ambitious furniture, or reclaiming and rebuilding other people's cast-offs. My late mother-in-law had a particularly keen eye for deconstructed curb-find furniture. She delivered a Victorian rocking chair to me one day, entirely dismantled and dumped into a cardboard box, some of the spindles splintered at the ends, painted in layers of eggshell, green, and yellow. I stripped all the paint to find that it was cherry. I repaired the spindles, then reassembled it, gluing it together in the complex Rubik's formula of chair assembly, a process for which six hands would be helpful, plus a lot more patience than I actually possess.

The chair now sits in a corner of Gina's and my bedroom, and it looks great, and it wobbles only a little if you don't count the right arm, which wobbles a lot.

But it's the process that I love, more than the product. And it's the process that I missed. I enjoy working on my house, but it's different than building furniture, as anyone with old plumbing can tell you. There's a lot of work and no glory in fixing a leaky bathtub drain, not to mention fixing the ceiling hole caused by the leak. As my dad once said of plumbing, "The only way anyone could tell you've done it right is if no one can tell you've done it at all."

As my dad and I slowed to a stop before a long aisle of vertically stacked boards, an old excitement took over, the thrill of the quest. The lumber was arranged in increasing increments of quality and price, from basic framing lumber to furniture-grade: pine to poplar to oak.

We'd figured to use midgrade pine, calculating that the ultimate purpose was somewhere between permanent and temporary. I stopped in front of the display of one-by-eights, stacked vertically. I pulled out the top piece, knowing full well it would not be the one I'd select. The top board on the stack is never any good, because it's always the one the last person put back, and there's always a reason. Lifting it and setting it aside is akin to opening the lid of the Cracker Jack box, ready for the hunt to begin.

Just in case, I sighted down its edge, and sure enough, it was not only warped but also chewed up along one corner.

I pulled out the next one and ran it through my hands. A knot showed through both sides. I set it aside.

More warped boards, more knots, more dinged corners. Eventually, I narrowed down the stack of maybes, aided by my father, who pointed out that any warping would be pulled straight in the process of joining the corners and edges. Finally, with sufficient certainty, I fed the best eight eight-foot planks into the rack on the orange steel cart.

We moved down the row toward the end, to the harder, richer vein of red oak, more expensive but also easier to negotiate. The grain was cleaner and the wood more fine, plus we knew we'd be ripping it into three-quarter-inch strips, so the whole face of any given board wouldn't show. We leaned half a dozen planks along the face of the display as I dug deeper and deeper.

I was doing my best to approximate some sort of organic connection, but inside I felt more than a little deflated. This wood, each piece affixed with a bar-code sticker, was soul-less, assembly-line lumber. A chef acquaintance of mine once described to me the process of preparing coq au vin. He said that the first step is to go to an organic chicken farm, carefully choose a rooster, give it a name, take it home, and feed it for a couple of days, talking to it in soothing tones not only so the bird is not stressed when you finally chop off its head, but also so there is an emotional investment that will carry over into the preparation and finally the meal itself, which, if executed properly, will honor both the bird (we'll call him Alfred) and the chef, the meal representing the crowning transaction in a brief yet rich affair.

I've always felt the same way about wood. Countless times—many of them in my dad's workshop, many in my own—I've dug and sorted, tapped and hand-weighed, sniffed and tested with a thumbnail for density and sometimes even tasted, seeking the one piece of wood that felt true to its purpose. A piece with some kind of blemish or oddity, with soul. I form meaningful relationships with my building materials.

One time, in the storage shed of a semiprofessional junk collector, I found a hunk of hard old oak salvaged from a door edge, and I offered the guy five bucks for it, pointing out that it had two holes in it.

"I usually charge extra for those," he intoned.

Another time, I dropped by my dad's barn in search of some weird piece of scrap lumber suitable for a little wine-stopper display holder I was concocting as a gift for Gina. I knew theoretically what I wanted, but I wouldn't know what I was looking for until I found it—the arch from an oak rocking chair leg. For a long, uncomfortable moment, my father hesitated, suddenly aware of its perfection, uncertain whether he wanted to let it go so easily. I get it. I can't even throw away the handles of broken brooms and shovels.

After my grandfather died, I inherited an ancient wooden box that used to sit in the old man's Geppetto-like workshop, an utterly fantastical place that was carpeted with a deep cushion of his cigarette butts and was as close as I will ever come to transport into the world of the Brothers Grimm.

The box now sits on a little table next to my desk, slightly battered, deep brown, neatly dovetailed at the corners. It is labeled on the front in faded black lettering pressed into the soft wood:

COMMERCIAL
WOODS OF THE
UNITED STATES
Prepared by
National Lumber Manufacturers
Association Washington, D.C.

Inside are forty-eight little rectangular blocks, each numbered and labeled with the wood's source, its properties, and its uses.

No. 45, for instance, is tupelo, which comes from "Virginia, Kentucky, southward and westward to Texas" and is useful for, among other things, "millwork, factory flooring, tobacco boxes and veneer."

No. 32, rock elm, of the "Lake States," makes fine automobile bodies, refrigerators, and (in a curious overgeneralization) "woodenware." Northern white cedar, No. 3, light in weight, soft, and easily split, is a fine choice for "posts, ties, poles, shingles and canoe ribs." Willow (No. 47) is good for "baskets, furniture and artificial limbs."

A number of the samples specify among their uses: "coffins." In each case, the suitability seems both logical and lyrical. Tidewater red cypress, for example (cypress, a symbol of mourning). And chestnut (not too heavy). And sap gum and red gum (both versions of eucalyptus, whose leaves are medicinal). And redwood and western red cedar (resistant to decay).

For all my fascination, however, there was no tidewater red cypress at Home Depot. No chestnut. No sap gum.

Trying to intoxicate myself with the scent of raw timber

here only reinforced that we were working with the Miller Lite of lumber. The ceremony would have to find its own way into the job.

We finished in the lumber aisle, rolled the cart back through the brightly lit store, stopping for a bottle of glue and small brushes to spread it. I grabbed a sixteen-foot tape measure that I spotted on sale and we rolled on to the checkout: $257.03.

11: THIS AIN'T NO PICNIC

One year before.

It was cold, and it was still dark, and we were standing in the parking lot of the high school that had graduated us three decades before.

Other reasons we shouldn't have been there:

Because it was a Saturday morning. Because it involved running. Because it involved running five *kilometers,* which I had recently calculated, to my dismay, to be in excess of three miles. The very word "kilometer" concerned me. It was a word that had been aborted, along with "milligram," "Celsius," and all the rest, when St. Hilary Elementary School gave up trying to teach us the metric system, a grand global experiment declared dead by the nuns.

Three-point-one miles seemed like a long and potentially painful stretch, and these particular 3.1 miles involved a hill that I didn't feel comfortable scaling in a car, in dry weather, much less on foot, on a late-March, much too early, very cold morning.

On a Saturday, no less. And we had paid *money* to be here. This was a fund-raiser for the church connected to our Catholic high school, celebrating its 175th anniversary, hence the sign-up fee: $17.50. When I had asked John early in the week if he wanted to join me and Gina, he responded dryly: "Running is free. I don't pay to run."

But here we were. We had paid. I had my hands wrapped around a travel mug of coffee, partly for warmth and partly for the delusion that if I held tightly to something, anything, it might save me from being dragged to the starting line. I was wearing insulated pants, and a thermal top, and a long-sleeved T-shirt, and a zip-up sweatshirt, and gloves, and a stocking cap. John was dressed in sweatpants and a bulky At the Drive-In hoodie and a bright green windbreaker and a Dodgers cap. We did not look fleet. We did not feel fleet.

I had been running some since the previous summer. Like most middle-aged people who begin this pursuit, I was more or less running *from* something. In this case, other people's cancer. First my mother's, and now John's and my dad's. One fact was becoming impossible to avoid: that I was not going to live forever and ought to be taking better care of my body, or at least that I ought to recognize I had the option to do certain things toward that notion. I was well. Suddenly, maybe for the first time in my life, I was distinctly aware of this fact and my good fortune within it. I was well. I wanted to stay that way. And so I'd been running. Some. My philosophy was that I was willing to run until it hurt but no further. So I didn't measure in miles. I measured in minutes. A half hour was my threshold. Long enough to listen to eight or nine songs on my iPod. Such was the strictness of my exercise regimen: half a Stooges album. I'd never run an organized 5K before this morning. And therefore I had no idea whether I was capable of running 3.1 miles.

John, on the other hand, had been jogging and going to the gym for a long time leading up to his illness. In a bullheaded attempt to take control and to prepare his body for the previous summer's surgery, he had covered nearly a hundred miles in the week before entering the hospital.

So the two of us, ever competitive, made a pretty even match: more or less healthy me versus cancer-recovery John.

Gina, John, and I wandered toward the entry gate to the football stadium, where a table was set up to distribute number bibs and safety pins. I leaned against a fence post to halfheartedly stretch my hamstring. Gina held her coffee mug with both gloved hands close to her face, trying to keep warm. John chatted with some high school friends. He and I had first met in this place, but it was really just a casual beginning point for a friendship that took its true hold in college. In high school we were something like friends, but John was something like friends with just about everyone in the school. He moved easily between cultures and discovered new ones. He wrote and distributed an underground publication called *Offbeat*, which of course we immediately began calling "Beatoff." John discovered graffiti on a railroad bridge near the school with "V-Nervz" spray-painted across its side, and upon investigation discovered that this was a local hardcore punk band, and then in his fanzine he announced their upcoming all-ages show at an underground venue called Club Hell, and soon we were Club Hell regulars. He found a way to be avant-garde even in a place as ordinary as ours.

John wandered back over to where Gina and I stood near the shuttered concessions stand, and he pulled out one of his standard catchphrases, mimicking the announcer who called our football games back when we were kids sneaking Mickey's Big Mouths into the stadium: "And the rest . . . of your 1982 . . . Fighting Irishhhhhhh!"

*   *   *

John had been improving steadily since the fall. He had begun painting again. In his basement workspace, amid the dense clutter of cheap pro-wrestler action figures, underground rock-show posters, old printing-press letters, and the like, he had been working with black and red ink on large sheets of vellum. He'd been unusually private about this. For a long time, I didn't even know it was happening. The two of us had a long history of trusting each other with work we had in progress. He read pieces of my writing before I showed them to an editor; I always saw his projects in their various stages before they became public. As we had for our whole lives together, we shared music and books. I would suggest music to him that I'd discovered by way of music he had suggested to me, which he had discovered by way of music I had suggested to him, and so on. John would buy a stack of CDs at the record shop in our neighborhood, then digitize them and sell them back to the same store, where they would be placed in the used bin. It became a running joke with the owner that whenever I would stop in and pull out a stack of used discs to buy, most would be from John's recent delivery.

We had been operating this way since we were teenagers. But this new endeavor of John's, this immersion in his artwork, seemed different. It seemed insular, almost hidden. I knew John wasn't sleeping much; it was hard for him to find a position that didn't make him feel like his guts were bubbling back up through an esophagus that no longer had a shutoff valve, and I knew there was something about his new work that was ambitious and urgent and probably desperate. He was using the ink and sheets of vellum to create a series of large 39-by-28-inch paintings loosely based on his experience during college working in a small rubber factory. A quarter century before, when Akron was still known as the Rubber Capital of the World, he'd done his senior project on this same subject. I'd helped him set it up in a janitor's closet he'd commandeered in the University of Akron art school, which he turned into an installation space where he created a multimedia show with film, photography, painting, and sculpture, all about factory culture. Visitors punched in at a time clock as the Minutemen's frantic two-minute punk rock song of the working life—"This Ain't No Picnic"—played on continuous loop, a crash of images and sounds forming an all-encompassing collage of John's experiences and ideas. The paintings he was making now derived from the dark mythologies of stag films and illegal drinking and gambling in the underground tunnels where the pipefitters worked; the macho, ball-busting insults of the lunch room; the weird chemicals and invented language that had stayed with John since then. As part of that senior project, he made a photo book titled "Hone That Bone," a crude jerk-off shout-out the men made to break up the boredom of their labor. And now this roiling, formative memory was coming out in work that was raw, dark, and energetic. The paintings were the size of movie posters. When the ink soaked into the vellum, which is sort of like parchment, it created a wrinkled effect, so each piece had a distinctly visceral feel.

When I'd stopped over to visit him on Christmas Eve, he insisted that I stay, and he fed me a plate of huevos rancheros and potatoes he'd cooked that morning, and he showed me some of the paintings. We went down the basement, and I was taken aback by just how much he'd been working. The scare of mortality was obvious here: this was as much as anything else a tangible display of the simple message he'd given me years before, sitting in Gina's and my kitchen: life is short. Now we had evidence.

We got our race numbers and pinned them to our fronts, on the top layer of clothes, then joined the cattle call making its way across the parking lot to the starting line. John still had trouble keeping up with his breath and had told me he'd probably be alternating between jogging and walking. This suited me just fine. I told him I'd keep to his pace.

We stood under leaden early-morning light, somewhere in the middle of a couple hundred people. Near the front stood serious runners angling for starting position, some holding one foot awkwardly behind them to stretch quad muscles, others leaning down at angles, bouncing lightly, some jogging in place. We who knew no such preparation kept ourselves at a safe distance, nestled more comfortably among the rear guard of complainers and coffee drinkers.

Someone up front said words we couldn't really hear, the parish priest gave a blessing, a starter's pistol fired, and we took off, jogging into a pace amid the nylon swish and early puffs of rhythmic breathing.

The first leg took us steeply down a hill, a paved street in an old roughed-up part of our hometown, the sidewalks scattered with gravel and bottle-glass kernels and random litter left behind from the snowplow piles. Over a set of railroad tracks, and then we crossed onto a picturesque national-park trail that followed the old Ohio & Erie Canal.

The clump of runners had stretched out, and the pace was quieter. We could hear the water's slow progress and the birds in the sketch of late-winter trees. We could see our breath. It burned now that my lungs were taking it in deeper, and as the course leveled off and John slowed to a walk, I did, too. I talked as John labored to get his wind back. Then he talked. He told me this had been part of his route before he got sick. He would take his lunch hour to run down through here, then power his way up an impossibly steep parkway. I'd never known this. For as much time as we spent together and as long as we'd been friends, there were always parts of John's life I didn't know about. He was naturally stoic. His heart was always guarded.

For years, much of our time together involved going out, to see bands in clubs, to art openings, to oddball events he would drag me to. In a particularly troubled spell of his marriage, he and I had gone up to Cleveland on a subzero night to see a C-grade Elvis imper-sonator who looked and acted more like Carmine "The Big Ragoo" Ragusa than the King of Rock and Roll, a night that as it progressed may as well have been a David Lynch short subject, ending with us returning to his pickup truck to find a frozen pigeon in the bed.

His new discipline translated to a new distance between us. He didn't drink. He didn't go out. Our once natural time together had dwindled. Our friendship had become about his illness and not much more. We both recognized this, so we'd been talking for a long time about setting up a standing breakfast date. This is how middle-aged friendships often go, slipping and slipping until "we really should get together soon" becomes a discomfort-ing veil for the truth—that such friendships cease to exist. While it seemed absurd, it also seemed obvious: we needed to schedule ourselves into each other's lives.

"We need to get this breakfast arrangement happening," I said as we continued walking.

"Can you do Tuesdays?"

"Yeah, I can do Tuesdays."

"Seven-thirty?"

I groaned. "Really? I guess if I had to."

John reached into his nylon pocket, pulled out his phone, and did something with the keypad. "It's done," he said. "We now have a scheduled breakfast date, second Tuesday of every month, seven-thirty, at Wally Waffle."

"What did you just do?"

"I set up an Outlook reminder."

To my low-tech self, it seemed as though he had performed some sort of digital alchemy. "I don't think that will work," I told John. "I don't use my phone."

"It'll come to your email account."

"Wow. That's like magic. Okay. So we'll be meeting for breakfast once a month?"

"Yep."

"Like old men."

"Yep."

Ten days later, an auto-generated Outlook Express reminder would chime, and a box would pop up on my computer screen: "WALLY WAFFLE TIME." An odd thing, to schedule time with your best friend this way. But it was a way to keep a connection that had been strained in the past year, a way to replace nights in bars and the planning of parties and countless afternoons drinking beer around a patio fireplace.

John was ready to run again, and we picked up our pace, jogging to the turnaround at the halfway point and making our way back through the trees, the cold canal dragging along at the same pace we were. We both groaned when we returned to the hill, which now we'd have to climb, and began our labored way back up. The final stretch led through the school parking lot and into the football stadium, where the runners completed half a lap before crossing the finish line. John and I entered the stadium, picking up our pace to a jog.

He broke into his announcer's voice: "And the rest . . . of your 1982 . . . Fighting Irish!"

We rounded the turn toward the finish line. I pulled ahead, looked back, grinned, and raised my arms in victory as I crossed the line before him.

John and I had our first breakfast at Wally Waffle, then a second and a third. He got us tickets to a Radiohead concert. We made plans to see Richard Lloyd of Television at a small local club.

My dad, meanwhile, was looking and feeling more and more like himself. The low droop in his lip—nerve damage from the tumor surgery—was easing back, hardly noticeable. He'd been exercising the muscle according to doctors' orders, and he was improving and improving. As springtime progressed, it almost seemed as though his recovery had been timed to prove that these milestones—him turning eighty; their fiftieth wedding anniversary—did not mark how old he was getting but how much time he had left.

And then my mom died in July.

"Your mother will talk to you in a dream," Gina said on one of those early days of confused, exhausted bereavement. She said this as a matter of fact from her own authority of grief; she had lost her parents a year apart not long before. People had told her this would happen, and it did. My mother, she said, would visit me in some way, and it would be real.

I was at that point far too self-absorbed to have any sort of space in my imagination for an apparition of my mother. In that early spell, her death was about me, not her. I was talking to my own self about it so much that she couldn't have gotten a word in edgewise. All the crying and all the listening to sad Rufus Wainwright songs left me fatigued. So did the neurotic math that I kept doing in my head, calculating and recalculating, for instance, that it had been three weeks and one day since her heart attack and seventy-six hours since she mouthed, "I love you" and thirty-eight days since the last time she was in my house, standing there on that fourth floorboard from the wall, and so on and so on. An internal obsessive compulsion to find logic, order, to make sense. It never worked. No matter how intricately I recalculated the sequence, there was still an infinite void at the end. Regardless of how carefully the facts and feelings were aligned, it always concluded with the same result: an insoluble mystery.

For weeks, all I did was feel sad. What I found was that feeling sad about death made me feel sad about everything. Feeling sad about death made me feel sad about my son winning a baseball award. It made me feel sad about a birthday cake. It made me feel sad about a sunset.

Feeling sad about death made me feel sad about everyone who was getting older, which is rather a slippery slope once you start doing that math. And it's also kind of selfish. I knew I was supposed to be celebrating her life instead of mourning her death, but I was having a hard time getting there. I kept wallowing in the notion that this event had happened to *me*.

So when John showed up that day of her funeral and toasted her with his first glass of wine, it suggested a new and better understanding. It was a slight but important gift that he didn't know he was giving me, and one I didn't realize I was receiving.

Three weeks after her funeral, John celebrated the opening of a solo art exhibit called *Pipefitters, Porn & P.B.R.* at an Akron gallery. The gallery's main room was filled with his paintings, the ones he'd been working on in his basement through the winter and spring. A second room was full of smaller mixed-media collages on the same themes, using materials and images he'd gathered over the years. It was clear he was using everything he'd stored up over a lifetime. The art told a narrative of the life John had lived in and around the old industrial city: A painting of a Ball jar labeled *Earl's Mercury*, based on a story he'd heard about a worker who smuggled chemicals out of the factory. A portrait of a grinning man running a reel-to-reel stag-film projector in the dark. A crumpled Lucky Strike cigarette pack. The show was not just an announcement of his return but an optimistic prediction that there was much more to be done. And there was.

The series included a single portrait of a former heavyweight boxing champion from Akron, Michael "Dynamite" Dokes. John had met Dokes by chance earlier that year in the bar of a downtown restaurant. They struck up a conversation that didn't end until several hours later, when John finally offered to drive him home. Dokes was energetic and gregarious and spilling over with bizarre anecdotes. He kept ordering drinks and appetizers, eating incessantly without benefit of silverware, telling his story. He'd had a great rise and a great fall, legendarily knocked out in a 1983 title fight at an arena just outside Akron, the final punch so brutal it broke the winner's hand. He'd had trouble with drugs, served jail time for attacking his girlfriend, lost much of his fortune. Now he, too, had cancer and was fighting it. John was fascinated with him and wanted to make a documentary about his life. The two men became friends, but the friendship quickly changed as Dokes's cancer advanced aggressively. Dokes died less than two weeks after the opening of the *Pipefitters* show.

John buried himself in yet more work, three months of intense activity to produce another series of ink-on-vellum works of the same scale, all about Dokes. He made a second series of small mixed-media collages called *Dynamite Vs.,* each depicting a Dokes opponent, labeled with the date of the fight and a brief note on the outcome: "Dynamite vs. John Lewis Gardner . . . June 12, 1981 . . . Joe Lewis Arena, Detroit, MI . . . Dokes knocked out England's John Gardner in the fourth round." The black-and-white photograph is overlaid with text from a boxing program, Dokes at the edge of the frame, cropped save for his round shoulder and round glove in recoil, in reload, a mesh grid layered over his eyes deepening their intensity, as the opponent falls backward, hair asunder, knees buckled, deadweight. Down.

The Dokes show opened Thanksgiving weekend amid a Saturday-night early-winter snowstorm, in two spaces in our neighborhood across the street from each other—a clothing boutique and an independent record shop with a gallery space. In John's usual throw-everything-into-the-pot approach, the evening included a soundtrack and a DJ, a handmade zine, stickers and fliers, a cooler of beer, the Dokes family in attendance, dozens and dozens of people trudging through the snow between the two galleries, filling the night with sound and heat and light.

I made my annual Christmas Eve visit to John's house to deliver a gift, the new Sufjan Stevens Christmas album, *Silver & Gold*, which I knew of only because he'd told me about it. He gave me one of the factory pieces, a painting of a pigeon with a crooked beak and a band on its leg and the word "Jim's" down in the shadowy corner because, as John explained, that was Jim's pigeon, a factory pet. And he gave me a bunch of new CDs he'd burned. I stuck them in the center console of my car, and they became the soundtrack of my winter and spring.

We had our standing breakfast date again in January, and as we sat at Wally Waffle, we made plans for a road trip to Pittsburgh in April to see the Black Keys, an Akron band we'd been seeing together since their first shows at a downtown club; they were now filling arenas. We were returning, and I was glad for that.

On my birthday, we shared our annual celebratory drink in a bar where John alternated between talking to me, on his left, and to the very pretty, very young woman on his right.

He turned to me.

"I think she's still in college," I said.

He turned back to her, then back to me, raised his glass of red wine, grinned, and offered a private toast, sotto voce: "Making mistakes . . . since 1964."

12: PATIENCE

I set out for my dad's house under a tired, white-cotton morning sky. I had to put the convertible top down to accommodate the eight-foot oak boards I'd stained at home, and I worried all the way there. This was a particular species of Ohio summer sky— not full enough for a good honest rain but too full to hold it all in. More often than not, it would randomly start spitting like a halfhearted water pistol. I drove a little faster, uneasily, to make it there before the boards got wet. Also, I felt more than a little foolish hauling lumber in a car entirely unsuited for the purpose.

I made it to his driveway without incident, shouldered the boards, and entered the barn. Dad, as always, was already in his place, dressed in a russet T-shirt and faded jeans, tinkering. In his cluttered, tool-strewn, sawdust-coated workshop, he'd begun setting up his bench router with a tongue-in-groove bit in preparation for the boards I was bringing. For all my interest and engagement with tools, the router was something I'd never been able to gain any real facility with. My own router was cheap and underpowered, and I'd burned up enough bits and mangled enough boards that I'd more or less given up on this particular aspect of woodworking.

But one of my goals with this endeavor was to learn from

him—practical skills and hopefully more. Whatever he would allow. And just to have a reason to spend extra time with him. While I knew he'd be taking charge, I set out deliberately to understand what he was doing. I wanted to follow each step, and I wanted to be allowed to perform as much of the hands-on part as possible.

But this router. Lord. A half hour in, I was beginning to think the reason I want my father to live forever is so I will be spared the tedium of setting up a tongue-in-groove bit. These kinds of joints are tricky, especially in boards so long. But when it was all finished, three pieces would (theoretically) fit together like a puzzle to form a wide plank: two wider lengths of white pine with a darker strip of red oak down their middle. It was beginning to feel like we were doing anything we could to make this simple box as complicated as possible. And by we, I mean him.

I stood on one side of the steel-legged bench across from my dad, who was hunched over the router, which he'd pulled free from its seat in the middle of the mounting bench. He squinted and pursed his lips as he turned the adjustment knob yet again, a fraction of a rotation, raising the height by just a hair. He locked the guide plate into place once more, then set the unit back in its spot at the center of the bench, adjusting its seating there. The exhaust fan filled the air with a hissing sound. The wall clock ticked. It was no coincidence that behind me, taped to the door-jamb, was a yellowed card in the shape of a dove, printed with a Bible quote, Romans 8:25: "If we hope for what we do not see, we wait for it with patience."

Finally, he flipped the switch. The hard whirring of the power tool overtook the room. With a careful hand, my father eased a scrap piece of pine along the featherboard—a guide with a series of flexible plastic tines, like the teeth of a giant comb if they were turned to 45 degrees—and he fed it into the sharp, spinning bit, its zipping whine chewing out the groove at twelve thousand rpm. A faint smell, like toasted oats, rose up. After running ten inches or so, he eased the piece of test lumber back toward him, then drew it away from the bit, switching off the motor.

He eyeballed it, blew dust out of the groove, then checked its depth with a little yellow plastic gauge. At last he declared we were on the money.

He turned and retrieved one of the long pine boards from the stack against the wall. He handed it to me. "I did the hard part. You get the glory," he said. He switched on the router motor.

I fed the board forward, feeling its vibration as it met the spinning steel.

"Ease off a little," my dad called over the motor. "You're pushing too hard."

I slowed. My dad left the room and returned with a tripod-looking thing, a set of angled red legs with a shiny steel roller on top.

I backed the board out and he set the tripod underneath. It supported the free end of the plank, enabling me to use both hands to control its movement through the router.

"I wish I was the genius who invented this thing," he said.

He may not have been the genius of its invention, but he was a savant of ownership. He had every tool one could imagine and a number of tools one could not—such as this rolling sawhorse—and yet I don't think he had any superfluous gadgets. (Or not many, anyway—he did own a branding iron with his initials.)

Slowly, my confidence and facility increased. I routed one board; it passed my father's inspection, he gave me a nod of approval, and I moved on to the next. I fed it through the guide, hot sawdust shooting out against my palm. An hour passed, then another. Eventually, I became one with the process, a transformation I've always savored. First one enters the work, then the work enters oneself.

I was feeling better, more independent, like I had learned enough that I could operate on my own, at least for now. I arranged the pieces of oak, and when my dad had calibrated the new bit and set the featherboard to its proper spacing, I took over again. I began to feed in the thinner piece of harder wood and immediately felt a distinct difference. The wood was denser, the grain less compliant, and its decreased width meant less stability on the bench's surface. The bit grabbed suddenly and yanked the board—and me—violently forward. The knuckles of my left hand jammed into the featherboard. My heart quickened and my skin tingled with shock and fear: if that barrier of plastic tines hadn't been in place, my fingers would have been shredded.

I killed the power. The bit stopped spinning. The two middle knuckles of my left hand were torn up and bleeding. A thick red smear stained the board I'd been feeding. I lowered my injured hand to my side, wiping the blood against the leg of my jeans and shaking it. My dad was watching.

"That thing can take over quick," he said. "Are you okay?"

"Yeah," I said, and I was inordinately sparked by the realization that I'd just gotten blood—my own blood—on a coffin—my own coffin. I spontaneously began scheming a plan to preserve this stain throughout the sanding and finishing process, and to arrange the boards in such a way that it would be visible. It's not everyone who can say he's got his own blood on his coffin. Or maybe it's not anyone. Except me. And maybe Nick Cave.

I rinsed my hand under the washtub spigot and squeezed the damaged knuckles with a paper towel till they stopped bleeding. I picked up the board to inspect for damage, with my dad looking on. We determined that no significant harm had been done, just a bit of a rough spot that could be corrected with some careful passes through the router. By we, I mean him. Without judgment but also without discussion, he took over the task. He fired up the router and began feathering with sweeping, intuitive strokes until it was right.

13: A MOMENT

I don't sleep properly, and sometimes for weeks at a time I hardly sleep at all, so my dreams are rare, and I often enter and exit them haphazardly—waking up in the middle, stirring in a haze of half-sleep, grasping for the tail of an interrupted story. All of this adds up to a confused interaction between my conscious and subconscious selves. I keep a notebook on my nightstand, which sometimes reads like the middle passages of *Flowers for Algernon*, crazy nonsense in often indecipherable script. I once awoke in the middle of a fitful sleep and furtively scrawled what I believe to be the words "floor shoes" so I wouldn't lose the important, fleeting epiphany, but to this day I do not know what it means.

This dream was different, however. It was the true depth of night, and I was in bed, the covers over my head, but I wasn't asleep. I began, in that hyperaware, obsessive-math sort of way, to wonder where and who my mother was in her life at exactly the moment I was in my life right then, early morning on the day she was forty-eight years, seven months, and one day old. In the way a fellow insomniac will probably understand, I spontaneously calculated the chronology—it would have been predawn, October 6, 1987. That was when she would have been exactly who I was at that same moment in her life.

I began to ask her questions. What did she feel like in the morning? Did she feel pain? Did she feel happy about the day ahead?

And she started to answer. Not directly, and not in an artificial talking-to-a-phantom scenario, but neither in an entirely imaginary exercise. It was some sort of intense connection that wasn't like anything I'd ever experienced. It was happening. Like Gina had said. My mother was communicating with me.

Her answer was that she never felt great in the morning, and she never thought too much about happiness in that way. In this strange wordless communication, she indicated who she was and what a life is about. And then I felt the same sensation of her eyes connecting with mine as I'd felt in the hospital, in that final moment when I knew for sure we were sharing a wavelength but soon she would be gone. She delivered a single phrase, then disappeared.

Don't become lonely.

14: COLLAGE

He was walking through the late-morning shade from the back of his small yard when I arrived. I'd been out for a run and had spontaneously turned in the direction of his house, a mile and a half from mine. Down the tree-lined hill, past the bungalows and Cape Cods, across the stretch of sidewalk where our kids once raced with sparklers in the night. I slowed as I came up his blacktopped driveway, and there he was, taking one small careful step, then another.

He was gaunt and gray, clothes cinched to fit. He was down sixty pounds from before he got sick. He looked older than his father. His glasses, chunky with clear plastic frames, now seemed too large, giving his head the effect of a caricature. He looked like a bug. Even though I'd been seeing him often, each new visit required a new way of seeing him, a recalibration of what I wanted to say, of what I should say, of what I could say. He saw me from across the hedge and held up his hand as if to say "wait" while he worked a breath into his lungs.

It still shocked me how fast this had happened, how fast it was continuing to happen. Less than six weeks after that birthday toast, John and I had taken a two-hour road trip to the Black Keys show in Pittsburgh. John drove, as always. But he was having a lot of discomfort in his chest and was popping ibu-profen at an alarming clip. He kept pulling his seat belt loose. I told him that if he wanted, I would drive home. "I might let you," he said.

This was the first time in a lifetime of such excursions when he'd ever offered to let someone else drive. As he took me to one of his favorite Pittsburgh stops—the funky old Primanti Bros. restaurant by the Allegheny River, for sandwiches overstuffed with coleslaw and french fries—and then to the huge, glossy Consol Energy Center for the concert, I noticed that John was repeatedly lagging behind me. Farther and farther. It was the first time since his recovery that I saw a hint of anything other than progress. He knew something wasn't right. With his usual diligence, he'd been gathering information from two differ-ent doctors, one in Akron and one in Cleveland, comparing it, trying to solve the puzzle of his own insides, to see if he could find the cheat code. Something like a moment of truth had arrived. As in the "Call me" text two years before, he let down his guard and revealed it to me that night as we drove. Something was wrong. He had a consultation scheduled for the following Monday.

He called me when he returned from the appointment, and swore me to secrecy. There were "cells"—he refused to call it anything else—taking over the lining of his lungs.

"I need you to keep my head straight," he said.

I promised him I would.

I loved him. I knew no matter what that I could rely on him. I'd always known that. I knew how much he loved Gina. The three of us were our own version of a family. We could complete each other's thoughts on matters of Evel Knievel, on Wilco's career trajectory, on tequila, on the history of our hometown—a hard place to love that we both loved fiercely—and on the epic nights we saw Hüsker Dü and Guided by Voices play in Cleveland, and the days we saw our children born. We had each turned to the other in every crisis and joy. We had marked together the curious map of growing up. We had made each other better.

He took another step.

I stood on his patio just outside the back door, waiting for him, sweat gathering under my bandana and at the center of my T-shirt now that I'd stopped moving. I didn't know if he was young or old. I didn't know if I was young or old. He took another step, then another. I sat. He arrived and sat, too, leaning forward, elbows on knees.

"Were you doing laps?" I joked.

He grinned and worked up an answer. "I walked ten feet. Have to keep moving. It's my exercise."

He sat back in his chair, working his way through labored breaths. This patio had been a center of our friendship for fifteen years. It was a gathering place, with a wood-burning chiminea at one end. A series of clay ones had come and gone, including a crumbling and oft-repaired number that John had christened "Ol' Never Quit." When it finally did quit, a group of us, regulars at John's backyard gatherings, took up a collection to buy him a fancy black aluminum model, which now sat here at the edge of the patio, full of ash.

Before us, perched on the electric meter box near the back door, was his home's only permanent fixture: a forty-ounce bottle of King Cobra malt liquor, which someone had brought over the night we celebrated the signing of John's divorce papers. From that moment it stayed there, a monument. When John hired a crew to install vinyl siding, he told the men the story of the bottle and issued strict instructions that it not be moved. They honored the request, reverently sliding the vinyl slats behind the bottle as they worked on that section.

"Hard to talk today," John said. "Yesterday was chemo."

"That's okay," I said. "Hey, guess what I found at the thrift store? The first three Joy Division records. Thirty cents apiece."

"Nice. You buy 'em?"

"Of course I did. But I don't know if it's right for Joy Division to make someone so happy."

After a while, we moved into the living room, where John had been spending his days and nights in a recliner, wrapped in a rumpled Captain America sleeping bag. It was freezing; John had been keeping the air conditioner cranked. A close family friend, an angel of sorts named DonnaLee Pollack who worked as a nurse in Texas, had traveled up to Ohio to be his caretaker, and the two of them binge-watched crap TV— *Duck Dynasty* and *Swamp People*—and movies checked out from the library.

DonnaLee was out on an errand. I moved her blanket aside and sat on the couch. John and I made small talk.

We never discussed my casket. It's something we would have discussed in different times, under different circumstances. But we didn't. He never knew about it. But I thought about that, about what would happen if he were involved, which he almost certainly would have been. If John and I were making a casket, we would decorate the shit out of it. We would put a window in the lid, or maybe a mirror, or one of those eyeholes from a hotel-room door. We would hand-paint it. We would line the inside with free verse or band stickers. We would make it play music whenever the lid opened. We would make it a shrine to something; who knows what? We would work our way through a lot of bad ideas.

John kept a pocket-size journal, and every day he made a point to write down an idea. It didn't matter what it was. It didn't matter if it was good. Some days it was just a line sketch; others it was a full project outline. He kept plugging. Always, every day. One of his catchphrases, adapted from Gertrude Stein's poem "Picasso," had become the title of his website: "Never not working."

When the time came to miss him—and it did, a month and two days later—I didn't know how. He was gone, but he was everywhere. Fishing blindly through the front seat console for a CD to play, I pulled out the stack of discs John had burned for me in December, and selected Radiohead's *The King of Limbs*, which I hadn't listened to yet, and there he was, giving it to me. Sitting in my desk chair, in whatever direction I turned: The funeral home memorial card, printed with his picture and the Serenity Prayer. The low-rent local semi-pro wrestling poster—"The Bushwhackers vs. the 7' Giant T. and Zoltan"; "Doink the Clown vs. Mystery Superstar"—of which he had an identical copy at his house. The megaphone on the floor by my filing cabinet, a birthday gift he'd eventually regret having given me. The matchbook from Corky's Thomastown Restaurant & Lounge. The framed photograph from his trip to Amsterdam, its white matte covered with his narrative of the journey, a dense, continuous stream of handwritten words that wraps around and around and finds me turning the frame in my hands, close to my face, turning and turning, reading his words, translating that lost language: ". . . have an Amstel, Mica, Marta (Austria), the Gambrinus pub, bean soup with chicken wrapped in a pancake (tortilla), walk, tallest building is my hotel, chocolate for Bridget, shoes for Salty, a lot of these guys look like the villains in the airport hijack movies . . ."

Grief is a collage, a bunch of vivid images thrown together without a clear order, leaving it to the viewer to decipher, only to discover that each image leads to a new one, which leads to another, endlessly elusive.

The future is the past crashing through the present, and it never stops crashing.

I have been Catholic all my life, so I am aware of the distinct, defining dryness of a Communion host. However, I have never known a dryness such as that which I experienced upon returning to my seat after receiving the Eucharist, knowing that when this line of communicants was finished, I would be walking up to that raised lectern to deliver the eulogy. (Why am I always stuck with the eulogy?) Between the dehydration of the previous night's grief drinking—what John used to call "a high-level meeting with Captain Jameson"—and the decongestant I'd taken that morning, and the thick summer heat, and now this Communion wafer, the inside of my mouth felt like I was trying to swallow a collie. I gulped hard and used my tongue to try to peel the stuck wheat disc off the roof of my mouth. My heart was racing. Communion ended, with one of the Eucharistic ministers in tears. It was awful. We stood.

The priest completed the post-Communion denouement, then instructed the packed church to please be seated. I was the only one standing, making my way past sets of knees toward the main aisle. I took slow, careful steps toward John's blue casket, my route entirely defined by its presence in front of the altar. Easing between its side and the front set of pews, I ascended the steps to the lectern, smoothed the pages I'd carried in my jacket pocket, took a long look over the roomful of faces, familiar and strange, waiting until I was certain I was ready, and I began.

My voice quavered. I'd known that would happen. And when it did, I turned my gaze toward the pale blue steel box that contained my friend. It gave him dignity, I thought, and it offered a sort of logic, order, something that made sense in a week filled with such a density of questions. It seemed settled.

When I finished speaking, I walked toward the crossing at the front of the nave, paused at the casket, and instinctively genuflected and crossed myself. The priest, a no-nonsense septuagenarian, was watching. I wondered if I'd blasphemed, directing my sign of the cross toward this steel container rather than the big wooden crucifix in the sanctuary off my left shoulder. I didn't care.

The city was deep into a hot, muggy spell, and everything and everyone was dripping in a ninety-three-degree July afternoon as they made their way through a line of lasagna and chicken, salad and homemade pizzelles, brought by the friends and family who gathered at Gina's and my house after the funeral. John's Italian roots were deep, as the overabundance attested. If one must die, one should do so amid old-country people.

A big white tent covered our backyard, an unmistakable and ironic likeness of the one that had been there just weeks before for our son's high school graduation party. I'd borrowed John's laptop and tapped into his iTunes earlier in the week to make a playlist for his calling hours—eighty songs, which felt like a perfunctory sketch, yet also tracked a life story—and I played it now on the stereo. Barry De Vorzon's "Theme from *The Warriors*" . . . the Jam's "Art School" . . . Steve Earle's "Over Yonder." It felt like a final collaboration.

His nieces and nephews played basketball on the ragged hoop in the driveway and batted yellow balloons across the yard, and the old Italian relatives sat and sipped their red wine. As the afternoon wore on, I wilted into a chair across from my dad. He was wearing what he'd worn to the service: a soft yellow summer shirt open at the collar, khakis, and casual shoes.

"It was sad when Jim died," he said of the brother he'd lost just a week before. "But he was eighty-nine years old, and if he didn't die this year, he would have died next year, or the year after . . . He lived a good long life. With John—it's a lot harder to take."

That's all he said. It was certainly the least hyperbolic thing that had been said that day, and also the most true.

Near the end, John and I were reduced to truncated exchanges of words in emails and visits, as though we were distilled to a code of our own making. His responses, especially, seemed like he was meting out the few words he had remaining. One night after having ordered out for Chinese, I sent John a note, and we shared what turned out to be our final written exchange:

Me: "Tonight's House of Hunan fortune cookie, reductive and aphoristic, yet true: Old friends make best friends."

John: "True my brother."

15 : ONWARD

On the morning my father was to leave for Frankfurt to begin a ten-day trip through Germany and France, a big cherry tree fell in his yard. He sent an email to inform me: "Can't do anything about it right now. It won't leave the place while I'm gone. Give me something to do when I get back."

His departure on this more or less spontaneous adventure at the invitation of two of his nieces seems now timed as a sort of juxtaposition—maybe even an affront—to my fixation with the mathematics of death. The day his party landed in Frankfurt was fourteen days before the first anniversary of my mom's death and seventeen days before John died. When they disembarked from the plane, a message was waiting. My dad's brother Jim, the father of the two nieces who were with him, had suffered a massive stroke. He would die nine days later.

My aunt's message from Ohio was to her daughters, no-nonsense and emphatic: my dad was under no circumstances allowed to change his plans. Her girls could decide on their own what to do. The daughters made hasty arrangements to fly back home. My dad continued on. If the roles were reversed, he said later, he'd have wanted Jim to have the time of his life.

And so he did. He'd prepared almost boyishly for this trip, buying a new pair of shoes and a walking-around bag which he called his "murse," claiming he was there to find a "Fifi," and if he did he might not come back. In truth, he had two specific destinations. The first was the Troyes Cathedral, the second oldest cathedral in France, a spiky edifice with stonework as busy as needlepoint and astounding stained glass dating as far back as the twelfth century, which was being restored by a cloister of nuns who reside in the monastery there, and whom he had been helping with a small fund-raising campaign back home. The second was his old army base, Anderson Barracks in Dexheim, which he hadn't seen in half a century.

He'd left his cell phone at home, intending to live fully in the moment. For the next ten days, his guides were a young grand-nephew and his wife, a military couple stationed in Frankfurt. Together, the group hiked tirelessly through cobblestone streets and hillsides across Germany and into France, eating and drinking, touring castles and cathedrals, visiting sidewalk cafés and beer gardens, through days sunny and pleasant. Each evening, my father returned to his hotel, a short walk from his hosts' house. He was the only guest in the place. Before turning in for the night, he made handwritten entries on notecards—a simple engineer-like record of what he'd seen and done that day, the meals he'd eaten, small observations.

> *Fri. To Karl & Nicole's*
> *Checked in Hotel St. Paulishof*
> *Went to Neuleiningen*
> *Visited old guys in man cave*
> *Drank wine & told lies*
> *Dinner @ Eubelius Schnitzel*

In the mornings, he chatted with the housekeeper, whom he'd befriended even though she spoke virtually no English and he spoke limited German. Then he set off up the road for the day's adventure.

He visited the World War I battlefield at Verdun. Drank cognac in Troyes. Posed next to a giant sculpture of a human foot in Trier. Toured the Anderson Barracks. Ate enough Weiner schnitzel that he returned five pounds heavier than when he left. Attended a two-hour Mass in an ancient Catholic church. Visited with the Mother Superior at Troyes Monastery, posing with her for a snapshot on the monastery steps.

Two days before my dad's return to Ohio, Jim died. Dad came home in time for Jim's funeral, then John's funeral six days later. I spent that whole summer measuring every milestone by these events—my mother's death, my uncle's death, my friend's death. I don't think he did this at all.

16: HIS MARGIN OF PROPHESY

Gina and I found ourselves taking turns causing each other to cry, and it became something like a parlor game between us. We got really good at it.

In the kitchen one morning, she asked if I remembered the night I'd spontaneously handed John an entire loaf of French bread from the counter because he was hungry, and how he'd set off toward home on his bicycle in the dark, munching away. Of course I remembered. We both started bawling.

I knew which songs would cause Gina to break down within two bars (Wilco's "Jesus, Etc." took only the first stroke of the violin), and I would play them on purpose.

When we deleted phone messages from the answering machine, we always had to save the one from John, the last one he'd left, and inevitably, one or the other of us would play it: "Hey. I wanted to remind you I have four tickets to the National tonight in Pittsburgh, plus Dirty Projectors. You can have all four if you want. Gimme a call. I'm not gonna make it to that show. But trying to find someone that may be able to use 'em."

And off we'd go again.

Sharing grief was uplifting in an unexpected way: she had lost him, too, and while lots of people had lost him, we were the only two people who had lost him in our own unique way, together, and so sharing his absence was a bond between us. Gina had made a big pot of Italian wedding soup at the point when John was barely able to swallow, and she had split it into two containers, one for him and one for us. We recognized the fact that now each of our freezers contained identical halves of that soup, in identical plastic containers, and for some reason that was a bridge of comfort. But it also made us elaborately sad. Eventually, knowing when the crying was coming actually made us laugh. But we still cried.

Everything that summer had drifted into limbo. In late August, my dad and I made a date to meet in his workshop for the first time since we'd routed the boards for the sides, and I was glad for the distraction, for something to do with my useless hands. Our next step was to join the boards, brushing glue into the grooves and along the tongues, fitting the whole puzzle together, clamping it tight.

When I entered his workshop that day, the midmorning summer sun was pouring through the only window, which in turn revealed the sky, enamel blue, sponged with lazy white islands of cloud. The sunlight spilled onto the workbench where my father stood over a half-finished birdhouse he was making for a friend, carved in the shape of a baseball player's head.

"Hey hey," he said without looking up.

"Hey hey," I said back.

He was holding the freshly glued bill of the cap where it met the forehead. He nodded toward the end of the workbench. "I made us some drawings."

Before him, masking-taped to a scrap of the test-stained oak, were two new graph-paper "Designer: ME" sheets. I set my

bagged sandwich and water bottle on the router table. Dad carefully laid the birdhouse aside and picked up a pencil, turning
to the sketches and using the pencil for a pointer as he began
explaining the plans. The first sheet contained three different
drawings: one labeled "PLAN VIEW/CORNER," showing how
the four corners would be formed with a lap joint; the next
showing how the "BOT. EDGE" would be fitted and trimmed;
and the last an elaborate detail of the decorative oak trim that
would wrap around all the corners.

"You've lost me," I said halfway through my dad's explanation.

He grinned. "Okay. We're getting ahead of ourselves. But
don't worry. You'll see."

I was at the point of no return regarding the question of
whose project this really was. It was not an entirely clean collaboration. But nothing with my father ever had been. I'd learned
so much from him, more than I could even quantify, but he'd
actively taught me very little. I'd learned because of a fascination for him and the ways he worked. I'd learned from watching
him and mimicking, and I'd learned what questions to ask and
how to ask them. Now that I was approaching fifty, I'd come to a
certain kind of peace that I would never equal his example and
would always need him as a guide for this kind of pursuit, but
there was also the constant nagging awareness that someday I
wouldn't have it.

A number of years before, I'd set out to replace the rotten
wood floor of a basement foyer with brick I'd scavenged from a
house that was being demolished. I'd thought my plan was pretty
brilliant. This foyer led into the yet-to-be-restored billiards
room of our ridiculous Tudor, and I had determined that the
brick floor would both solve the issue of decay and offer a stately

rusticity to the wide cherry-trimmed hallway. While I hauled brick and figured a way to pour a concrete pad, my dad stopped by with a sketch of a brick pattern adapted and improved upon from a photograph he'd seen of a Spanish wine cellar, and it was far more intricate and interesting than anything I was capable of imagining. I was planning on a basic running bond, which is to bricklaying what chopsticks is to piano playing; his plan was more like modal jazz. Which meant that the floor would be better than anything I could have done on my own but also that it was no longer mine. He was right down there with me in high rubber boots with a shovel the day I poured the concrete subfloor. And I did learn. I realized this a year later when I rebuilt a set of brick steps and applied the arcane tricks of mortar mixing and bidirectional leveling and joint spacing, all things I'd learned from him.

Dad had laid out a set of the routed boards in their prescribed order across a pair of workbenches. Two eight-foot-long pine boards, eight inches wide, with a three-quarter-inch strip of the stained red oak in between.

"We have a little problem," Dad said, directing my attention to this arrangement. "Somehow we cut one of the boards an eighth of an inch short."

"How did we do that?"

"I don't know. I think we confused ourselves."

"What do we do about it?" I asked.

"Well, the beauty of this is no one will ever be able to see the front and back at the same time," he said. "We'll trim as best we can and chalk it up to imperfection."

Dad had a long wall rack for his dozens of clamps, which he'd fashioned from a length of black iron pipe. It displayed a wide constellation: short steel C-clamps; long iron and steel furniture clamps with orange rubber protective covers on their ends, some with threaded hand cranks, others with triggers that guided the ends toward tightness. Our first task was to raid it for all the long furniture clamps, laying them out along the span of the first set of boards so we could apply them quickly once the glue was spread. I picked up the big bottle of carpenter's glue and shook it upside down to move the viscous yellow fluid toward the spout. Dad grabbed two clean glue brushes and handed one to me.

"Ready?" he said.

"Yep," I said.

"We'll need to move fast. It'll start setting up quick."

He held one of the pine boards on edge, and I applied a bead of glue. He followed with his brush, spreading it evenly. We continued the whole length of each board, working briskly. When everything was evenly coated with glue, we clamped the three pieces together. Excess glue began to ooze from the joints.

"Not too tight yet," Dad said. "We want to get all the clamps in place and then tighten uniformly."

The hodgepodge battery of clamps found their places. Some of these clamps had been in his arsenal for as long as I could remember—heavy lengths of iron pipe with orange sliding tails and round black cranks. Others were much newer, shiny steel with fancy plastic triggers. He'd accumulated his tools over the years, as the countless jobs themselves accumulated. His current favorite was one he'd inherited from his brother Jim.

My own workshop at home reflected a similar history, stacked, jumbled, and adorned with tools from my childhood: a Boy Scout hatchet, my first framing square—and tools I'd bought for specific jobs: a power planer for my many ill-fitting doors, a rubber mallet for bricklaying—and tools my dad had passed down: a heavy steel pipe wrench, a string level—and tools from my grandfather: a machete, a meat saw—along with a few I'd borrowed from my father and brothers and hadn't (yet) returned.

As the boards slowly pulled together, the final fit taking shape, the imperfections revealed themselves. One stretch of board contained a gap where the pieces didn't meet cleanly.

"Wood filler," I joked.

Dad scowled. "Not if my name's going on it."

We cranked harder on that section and the gap began to disappear. But we also saw that the whole configuration was beginning to bow from the pressure.

"We're gonna need to strap some stout boards crosswise and clamp them down to keep it flat," he said.

We were fighting this thing in multiple dimensions, trying to make it parallel and true even as it heaved and kicked and angled in resistance. Dad quickly rooted through his boxes of scrap lumber to locate appropriate pieces, long and stout, to force it flat and level. Before working them into place, we cleaned the excess glue as best we could with sopping handfuls of paper towels. Then we set the boards perpendicular to the joints and pulled them tight with C-clamps, the wood groaning in protest as we forced it to go the way we wanted it to go.

We were out of clamps and out of floor space. Nothing more could be done for now.

"Let's walk away from this before we get too fussy," Dad said. "We can do the other one tomorrow."

I returned the next day. Dad had come out in the morning and removed the clamps. The iron pipes had stained the soft wood where we'd soaked it in our glue-wiping process, leaving streaks of gray. In addition, there were a few yellow-brown patches of dried glue we'd missed. I asked if that was okay. My dad nodded.

"You'll be doing plenty of sanding," he said.

For all the roughness, though, a significant transformation had occurred. These were no longer sticks and planks, the bones of an idea. This was what the side of the box would look like, and it felt like progress.

The following morning, I settled in at my desk in the old servants' quarters at home to catch up on email. When I opened Outlook, the little chime dinged. A notification box appeared on the upper right corner of the screen.

WALLY WAFFLE TIME
2 hours 12 minutes late

This was the second Tuesday of the first month since John had died. The app for our standing breakfast date was still active.

I could have clicked the "dismiss" button, but I didn't. I left it there. The reminder contained a strange and private communication between John and me, and I could find nothing within myself other than a desire to preserve it. It may have been a glitch of digital memory, a ghost in the machine, but I also knew that it was the direct product of his fingers on the buttons of his smartphone as we walked side by side along the canal that cold March morning sixteen months before.

I started into the mundane task of churning through email. Every time I returned to the Outlook window, the notification refreshed, chiming and reappearing at the top of the screen. I couldn't help but wonder if this was a version of Gina's promise that the departed speak to us in dreams. I chose again not to dismiss it.

As I cleaned out my inbox, I came across a Google alert. My name had appeared in a post somewhere. I followed the link to discover a puzzling version of a feature-length obituary that had appeared in the *Akron Beacon Journal* the week John died.

The original lead was this:

"John M. Puglia saw beauty everywhere, then created art from what he saw.

"From old factories to backstreet bars to boxers, Mr. Puglia was always moved by whatever came into his field of vision and continuously inspired others with his art."

But through some bizarre mutation of artificial intelligence, it had shown up on a secondary newsfeed, apparently after having been run through some version of autocorrect, and it came out looking like it had been translated into Chinese and then back into English:

"John M. Puglia saw beauty everywhere, afterwards total art from what he saw.

"From aged factories to backstreet bars to boxers, Mr. Puglia was always changed by whatever came into his margin of prophesy and invariably desirous others with his art."

I had been quoted in the original article, identified as "longtime friend David Giffels, a former *Beacon Journal* columnist and now an assistant professor of English at UA."

Now I was "longtime crony David Giffels, a former *Beacon Journal* columnist and now an partner highbrow of English during UA," and I considered John "a many exhaustible chairman."

I was quoted as follows:

"John lived an desirous life, and he desirous all of us who lived it alongside him. His possess continuous oddity and creativity led us into places we never would have gone. He took me into deserted factories and dive bars and peculiar corners of a cities we explored together. He introduced me to art and song and novel we wouldn't have found otherwise . . .

"He engrossed so much of life—art and film and song and novel and booze and sharp food and large ideas and stupid jokes—and he gave behind in equal measure. He common all he had."

There is no doubt in my mind that if John *were* to speak to me from beyond the grave, this was how he would have done so. We were well bonded in this kind of mischief. He once threw an elaborate backyard party to celebrate the art world's discovery of a previously unknown primitive artist named Dick Tappan. John had gone to Big Lots and bought a bunch of red apple Christmas ornaments and cheap wooden knickknack boxes with flowers painted on them, and had autographed them all with "Dick Tappan" in silver Sharpie. He'd developed a folk-hero backstory for Tappan and announced at the party that he would be giving each guest an original piece of the man's work. It wasn't until he handed me a megaphone for the announcements that the joke began to reveal itself.

"Everyone make sure you get your Dick Tappan . . ."

"This will be your only chance to get your very own Dick Tappan . . ."

"Remember, it's not a party until everyone has a Dick Tappan . . ."

And so forth.

All men, having once been thirteen-year-old boys, will forever after be thirteen-year-old boys.

I returned to my dad's workshop later in the week. He had some appointments that day and wouldn't be home, so he had left the barn open for me.

The boards we'd glued were stacked together vertically against the wall. They were uneven, bruised from the clamps, and stained from the glue. But they offered the scale of what they were to become.

I'd brought my power planer with me, and I set it, along with my bagged lunch, on the workbench. I was glad to be alone here, alone anywhere, with something to do. I wanted to clear my head, to give myself over to the slow rhythm of thoughtless work. The workshop felt wholly different without my father in it. I'd rarely—maybe never—been here alone, and in some way my presence felt like a violation of a private space. But it also felt like a privilege, a tacit trust.

I carried one of the two long sides to the sawhorses and lowered it into place. I plugged in the planer, tested the trigger, then stepped back to eyeball the general landscape. The seams between the wide pine boards and the thin oak racing stripe—as I'd come to call it—didn't match. In addition, there was some slight cupping in the pine that would need to be brought level.

I triggered the planer, the torque of which caused it to rotate slightly in my hand. The blade bit into the grain. Its pitch rose. It left a clean white wake as it removed a small fraction of the surface. Slowly, I made my way down the length of the board, sweetness rising from the young wood, a release of whatever it held inside.

Gradually and then completely, my mind was absorbed into the high whine of the little motor. I was transported into the task. When I found a need for a greater attack, I switched to my old-fashioned hand planer, sliding it along the high spots, leaving papery curls of wood trailing up out of the opening behind the sharp blade. Then back to the power tool. After two or three hours, I switched to my dad's disc sander to begin the finer smoothing. Sculptors will tell you that they allow a piece of stone or wood to suggest what it wishes to become, and even in the case of commercial-grade off-the-rack lumber, this communication was taking place. The wood's grain had determined which side would be inside and which would face out. The various pieces placed in proximity had suggested which ones wanted to match up. I was reminded, as one hour stretched into the next, of how John's work had taken him into the same sort of relationship with his medium, as he learned the way the vellum would respond to the ink, and he responded in turn, adapting his idea to that of his materials.

Late that day, as my work was winding down, my nephew Edward, a strapping sixteen-year-old in a straw fedora and Bermuda shorts, arrived to mow my dad's lawn with the old green tractor. I caught sight of him from the corner of my eye and shut off the sander.

"Workin' on your coffin?" he said, staring at the wood and nodding. "That's pretty cool."

"I guess so," I said, still unsure how to respond to such questions. Edward disappeared back into the other side of the barn, and I settled into the final round of sanding.

When I emerged a short while later into the bright sunshine of late afternoon, Edward was standing next to the tractor in the middle of the big yard, staring at it, thumb and forefinger of one hand stroking his chin. He saw me approach. "I shut it off and now it won't start," he said.

"Hmmm," I said.

I climbed into the seat, set my left boot against the clutch, and turned the key.

Nothing.

Now I stared with the same blank bewilderment. An old thought that had recurred countless hundreds of times since my dad's cancer arrived again: How will I do any of this without him? How will any of us?

I tried the key again. No response. Then a thought. "Was the mower running?" I asked.

"Yeah. I think so."

I reached for the black plastic knob and pulled the lever toward me, disengaging the blades.

Then, foot back against the clutch, choke pulled out slightly, I tried the ignition. BRRRRROOOMM.

Edward smiled, relieved.

"I knew it was something like that," he said.

"Yeah. Me, too."

Summer was ending. In some ways this had seemed like the worst season of my life, but the summer had also included Gina's and my twenty-fifth anniversary, celebrated with a trip to New York, and possibly the best (and definitely the most expensive) restaurant dinner we'd ever shared, at one of Mario Batali's restaurants—

Babbo, across the street from Washington Square Hotel, John's hotel—where the house music had unfolded as a seemingly personalized soundtrack of our decades together: Gina's and mine, and John's and mine, and Gina's and John's and mine. Over the long course of the meal, three albums were played in their entirety, each specifically meaningful to us in each of those decades—first the Pixies' *Doolittle* from the eighties, then Wilco's *Summerteeth* from the nineties, then the White Stripes' *White Blood Cells* from the aughts. This summer had also included the celebration of Evan's high school graduation—a boy growing to a man—and the vicarious sharing of my dad's trip to Europe—a man returning to his youth—and a great deal of goodwill from people who knew we were grieving.

On the last August Saturday before school started up again, Gina and I went to a screening downtown of a 1924 Soviet sci-fi silent movie—*Aelita: Queen of Mars*—that a bunch of local musicians had collectively composed a soundtrack for. I'd recorded a segment with a friend. (He'd provided the actual musicianship, scoring and synchronizing a looping melody. I'd accompanied him with the only movie-soundtrack guitar trick I know: a twangy riff drenched in vibrato and reverb, the ranch dressing of guitar effects.) Each of the participants had been given a three-minute excerpt to score, and the pieces unfolded one into the next into the next, creating their own spontaneity of performance against the black-and-white film. Taken as a whole, it was captivating and unexpectedly coherent, especially considering that many of the musicians had never met. Gina and I sat together in the dark and watched and listened, the accidental beauty of collage.

Later, we went to a big outdoor after-party. The organizers

had gotten permission from the owner of West Hill Hardware to use the parking lot behind his store for a bonfire gathering, with the store's cluttered back porch serving as a DJ stage. Someone had draped haphazard strings of Christmas lights along the rear of the store and around the parking lot. Some of the musicians who'd scored the film now created a live pastiche of electronica. Gina and I sat side by side on a pair of West Hill secondhand commodes stored next to the garage, passing a bottle of wine back and forth as we watched kids dancing in the firelight in their dreadlocks and gypsy dresses.

It was strange to see this on the site of the old hardware store. The party seemed either too modern or too primitive, generally too intentionally capricious for such a place. Nonetheless, I liked that it was here. I liked that I was here. I liked that I was here with Gina, slightly happy, slightly drunk, sitting on a toilet in this place that felt like home.

I looked up at the sky. It was black, starless, with an orange wedge of moon hanging aloof to one side. I was reminded of summer nights long ago, lying haphazardly on the dewy grass with my brothers and sister as my dad reclined in his plastic-webbed lawn chair, gazing upward, narrating the constellations, describing bears and arrows and the edges of the Milky Way. He knew all the shapes and names.

Directly above us, high in the blackness, was a constant swirl—the white undersides of birds, circling, swooping, down, up, a loose tornado of flight. They followed a chaotic pattern like bats would, but these were not bats. They were white. We lived barely a mile away, and I'd never seen this sort of bird activity in my own little piece of the same night sky. They were graceful and busy and constant. For the rest of that night, I wondered about them, why they were here, how they belonged. Were they attracted by the light from the fire, or the Christmas lights, or was it the music? Or were they always here, and I'd just never looked at the sky this way?

"I miss John," Gina said.

I hadn't been thinking that, but immediately, I agreed, and now I was thinking only that. "I know. He would have been here."

"He would."

PART 3

17: TURNING FIFTY

I have always been age-obsessed. Not in the vain way, necessarily—I don't mind that my body is aging, and the older I get, the more thankful I am for my years. But at every age since I can remember, I've tested myself against any potentially quantifiable benchmark. When I was nineteen, I was irrationally aware that Tommy Stinson, the bass player for the Replacements, was two years younger than I was and had already been a legitimate (or at least illegitimate) rock star for three years; I was also irrationally aware that he had made out with two girls I had also kissed, and at that point in my somewhat pathetic life, I'd properly kissed only four girls. My statistical analysis suggested two things: 1) Extrapolated across the fifty states, Tommy Stinson was getting a *lot* of action; and 2) I was already too old to become a rock star.

When I was twenty-six and finishing my master's degree in creative writing, I was irrationally aware that Michael Chabon was just ten months older than I was (actually, nine months and three weeks, but who was counting?) and had published *The Mysteries of Pittsburgh* two years before, which established him as a sort of literary golden boy, and that his writing shamed everything in my not even finished master's thesis, and therefore I was doomed before I'd even begun. Complicating matters that year was the fact that one of my professors returned from a trip to New Orleans with a gift for me, a copy of John Kennedy Toole's *The Neon Bible,* which had just been published twenty years after the author's suicide. This professor, who thought of me as a young writer, told me he thought I'd like to read the work of another young writer. But Toole had written the book when he was sixteen and had died at age thirty, and I was acutely aware that I was much closer to the latter than the former.

When I did turn thirty, I tacked a photocopy of Katha Pollitt's poem "Turning Thirty" to the wall above my writing desk (I am nothing if not literal) and therefore day after day I was reminded that I'd reached the age

when suddenly "choices"
ceased to mean "infinite possibilities"

This poem came from her collection *Antarctic Traveller,* and for a bookmark, I used the brochure I'd requested from the Anchorage "Star of the North" Chamber of Commerce. One of my recent infinite possibilities had involved a plan to move to Alaska, which was progressing swimmingly until Gina, who was unaware of the plan, discovered said brochure and informed me that, no, we would not be moving to Alaska. I responded by asking her if we could have a pet monkey. She said no.

My infinite possibilities continued to dwindle.

Mostly by chance, the first book I read for pleasure after completing graduate school was Douglas Coupland's *Generation X.* (A side note: isn't it the kind of irony that seems tailor-made for an English major that one becomes an English major because one loves to read for pleasure, and then, upon entering the major, finds that reading suddenly becomes anything but pleasurable?) That book accompanied a growing fascination with my age in comparison to the ages of others in my generation: what we had done, what we had failed to do, in our thoughts and in our words, forever and ever world without end amen.

The obsession continued. In my early days of using Facebook, when everyone still included a username as the opening phrase of a post, I declared one day that David Giffels "is younger than Johnny Depp, but feels older, and older than Brett Favre, but feels younger." I was finding myself unavoidably in middle age but at a complete loss to reconcile just exactly what that meant. Was I becoming less young or more old? Was I acting the way I was supposed to act? Was everyone else?

I thought a time would come when I would feel definitively like a grown-up, like I would have achieved a certain kind of acumen for making decisions and knowing what to do in unknowable situations, when I wouldn't feel insecure in real-life grown-up scenarios (board meetings; ordering wine; delivering eulogies). Instead, I still felt like a kid. Or rather, I felt like an adult who was in the continuous loop of his youth. I found my forty-four-year-old self at the mall one day with my tween-aged children, shopping for a pair of sneakers and wondering at their open contempt as I lingered over a pair of Chuck Taylors.

Dad. You're not cool.

Did they not understand that these were the only sneakers I ever wore, or had ever worn, and therefore my continuity undermined any accusation that I was trying to achieve hipness, to pass as relevant? I was simply trying to maintain a much valued status quo, and I specifically chose a white pair, the most pure and unstudied of all the colors, to drive that point home.

When you're twenty-four and buying Chuck Taylors, you strive to be incredible. When you're forty-four and buying Chuck Taylors, you strive to be credible.

Is this too much to hope for?

I've always loved music more than almost anything else, and especially discovering new music, which was a consistent and often glorious touchstone of my life with John. Yet when I was in my twenties and professionally wanted more than anything to become a rock critic, I also developed an inflexible theory that no one should become a rock critic after age thirty, such that when I was actually offered the position of rock critic at the newspaper where I worked at age thirty-four, I turned it down. Yet at the same time, I felt no discomfort continuing hungrily to seek and consume and talk about the newest music and the most obscure older music, which—a fact somehow lost on me— is precisely the job description of a rock critic.

Right in the middle of this uncertainty, at the age of twenty-nine, I made a more or less accidental connection with Mike Judge, who was, most important in this context, thirty. He was also the creator of *Beavis and Butt-Head*. The cartoon had just hooked into the cultural consciousness, and MTV wanted to ram it forward into mass production. Our meeting happened almost entirely by chance. I was a columnist at a small Ohio newspaper. *Beavis and Butt-Head* had suddenly become controversial (and huge) after an Ohio mother blamed Beavis's pyromania for leading her five-year-old son to start a fire that took the life of his younger sister. It was tragic, but it seemed to me that the parent was wrongly deflecting blame. I wrote something about this and, on a whim, sent it and another piece I'd written about the show to Mike Judge, care of a generic address I found for MTV Networks on the label of a promotional package that had been mailed to the newspaper's entertainment editor. Pretty much a message in a bottle.

A few days later, I received a handwritten note:

Dear David,

Thanks a lot for sending me your articles. I showed "Tooning in to the news" to everyone. It's funny as hell. It's been a rough couple of weeks and it was great to read something like that. In fact, if you ever want to try writing a B+B episode, let me know. You could make 500 dollars huh-huh-huh.

—Mike Judge

He included his phone number. I called him and we talked, and soon I was learning how to write a TV script by copying from the samples he sent me. He took the first idea I pitched, an episode called "Hard Sell," and I continued to contribute in a small way throughout the show's mid-nineties run. I wrote a Cornholio episode, and one of the Christmas specials, and a few others. I was not a major contributor by any means—rather, a cog in a big and busy machine. It was something I did mostly for fun. I pitched regularly, had ongoing conversations with Judge and Kristofor Brown—the head writer and producer whose humor, earnestness, and organization were a secret weapon behind the show's success.

The part of the experience that had the most lasting personal effect was also the smallest and most mundane: talking on the phone to Judge occasionally about the other parts of our lives, the parts that had to do with being regular-guy sort-of grown-ups.

We were both married. He'd recently become father to a second child; my wife was pregnant with our first. We both had a habit of perpetually fiddling with our wedding rings, and shared the consequent madcap tales of chasing them when they popped onto the ground. I was living in my native Ohio; he was wishing he could get away from New York and back to Texas, where he felt at home. We'd both played in bands while also experiencing the awkward transition into our early professional careers. He'd worked in an office and hated it. This was the inspiration for the cubicle drone Milton, Judge's first foray into animation, and the seed material for *Office Space,* which in retrospect seems more than semiautobiographical.

When we were chatting, I'm sure we sounded far more like Hank Hill and Boomhauer than Beavis and Butt-Head. We once had a conversation about the best way to set a fence post.

And now I realize there isn't much difference between those cartoon friendships and those of our real lives. In middle age, stuff still sucks, and stuff's still cool, and life goes on, but it doesn't, but it does.

This experience helped me understand what felt normal about being thirty, but also introduced the unique modern complexity of American adulthood. The thing Judge always understood best about his characters, and maintained so deftly, was that he wasn't writing for teenage boys. He was writing for the men those teenage boys had become and always were: us.

Some fifteen years later, MTV enlisted Judge to produce a season of new episodes. Beavis and Butt-Head were still fifteenish, and we kept getting older, but we also kept being the same. I watched those new episodes with my sixteen-year-old son, each of us occupying an end of the living room couch, slouched, wordlessly chuckling. Huh. Huh.

Simple math might not be the right measure for this generation of middle-aged American middle-class males whose culture has always been defined by stuff that sucks and stuff that's cool. I find myself amid the first wave of first-world men for whom the notion of a midlife crisis is irrelevant, because we don't really know how old we are. First-generation Black Sabbath fans are entering nursing homes with their heads full of "War Pigs." It's not that we're in a state of arrested development or denial but, rather, a legitimate temporal disorientation.

If my father had wanted to listen to the same music I was listening to when I was a teenager, he would have to do as I had done—painstakingly turn the coat-hanger-enhanced boom box antenna toward Cleveland in order to pick up the distant college rock station signal and then, upon learning that, say, the Meat Puppets were playing an all-ages show at a homemade underground club, going to the show because that was the only place to buy their record.

Now these experiences are delivered through the same machine I clock into every day when I go to work, and nothing seems absurd or desperate about such access. The new Best Coast record is there upon log-in, whether I'm searching or not. If the Velvet Underground had been delivered automatically through drill presses in midwestern machine shops in 1968, our world would be a very different place indeed.

In the modern world, my peers and I can't measure our career span against our target retirement date, because we don't really believe we'll ever retire. We can't claim existential alienation from technology, because it's inextricable from existence. We can't complain our bodies are breaking down, because science will no longer let them. We have been groomed to live out not the days of our lives but, rather, the days of our lifestyles.

R.E.M. broke up in 2011 to preserve their cultural credibility, as the Rolling Stones announced new tour dates for the very same reason, and what should represent a paradox instead feels entirely correct.

When I turned thirty, I kept trying to figure out if I *felt* thirty. I couldn't tell. When I turned forty, I didn't feel a decade older than thirty, nor a decade younger than fifty. Instead, I felt a chronological void, like maybe math was the wrong application. On that very day, my fortieth birthday, in New York City with John, I got carded by the barmaid at CBGB's, the fountainhead of punk rock. I gleefully complied.

And so, as my fiftieth birthday approached, I became consumed by a central truth: that I was arriving at a confounding and fascinating landmark that John and I should have reached together but never would. And that we would no longer be able to measure ourselves against each other.

What I did instead was set out to celebrate deliberately. Not to celebrate my birthday so much as to celebrate what I'd been given in life and what I still had. Grief has a way of becoming about everything in one's daily existence, and that had been the case with me and Gina for the past eight months. Everything bathed in the sadness of loss. We who are new to this experience are warned that the holidays are hard, and I expected that, and yet when the feeling hit, it came in completely unexpected ways. A few nights before Christmas, I found myself curled in a ball on the living room couch, crying inconsolably for two hours, a blindside meltdown triggered by happening unprepared across a photograph of me and John sitting together on my patio, smiling for the camera. I cried so hard that night that I was actually sore the next day, as though I'd been exercising. And yet in that same state, I felt a small catharsis, as though I had somehow given difficult passage to one of the great gallstones of mourning inside of me.

Part of this clunky and enigmatic evolution had come by way of the other sudden central development: at Thanksgiving time, my father revealed that he had been diagnosed with a lung tumor. At first this dragged me further down the rabbit hole of mortality obsession, until I accompanied him for a long day of tests and consultations with doctors at the Cleveland Clinic, where one message was pervasive, profound, and impossible to ignore. Over and over, he was told how fortunate he was, at age eighty-one, to be so vibrant and healthy. None of the nurses or interns or receptionists that day believed him when he answered (over and over) the hospital standard, "What's your date of birth?" He was living in a particular time—when a tumor in an otherwise sound body can be treated aggressively with an astounding modern arsenal and great optimism for recovery—and a particular place—under thirty minutes from one of the world's premier hospitals—and in a particular body that had, among my friends, earned him the nickname Iron Man, a body that would allow him to take on the most extreme radiation treatment available.

So where John, whom I thought of as young, had left me with the dark concern of vulnerability, my father, who was one of the oldest people I knew, offered a hopeful counterpoint: he was entering this strange new year as the most alive person I knew.

During a family dinner at our house one evening that winter, he said he was not afraid to die. He didn't say this in a philosophical, or maudlin, or resigned, or courageous way. Rather, he said, he'd done in life what he'd wanted to do, and now he felt like he was being given the gift of extra days and would repay that gift by making the most of them. He had begun telling more and more stories about his past, more and more candidly—about women he'd chased and women who'd chased him, mischief he'd gotten into and mischief he'd caused. I'd always known he'd dated a Playboy Bunny, but I'd never heard the whole story, which, honestly, once you got past the lead, wasn't all that much.

And it wasn't until that winter, after half a century with him, that I learned the story of his Army Corps of Engineers battalion building a bridge across the Rhine. How does a man get this far into life without knowing his father built a bridge across the Rhine River?

As someone who had always been fascinated by bridges, who had designed and built a countless number of them, many of them more impressive and certainly more permanent than that one, he may have just never considered the Rhine bridge particularly noteworthy. But still, we sat together, Gina and I and our kids, and observed the growing delight in his face as it dawned on him that, yes, this was a story worth telling.

In 1957 the 17th Armored Engineer Battalion constructed a temporary floating bridge across the Rhine, spanning about a quarter of a mile. More than a thousand men got to work on a Saturday afternoon, using air compressors to inflate canvas pontoons. These were then outfitted with metal saddles and

deck runners. At midnight, the Rhine was closed to water traffic, and the soldiers got to work. An advance crew stretched a
cable to the opposite side of the river, and the men began using a
bulldozer to feed one pontoon after another into the water. Each
piece was attached to the next by a heavy pin, driven in with a
sledgehammer. The men worked through the night into the next
morning, slowly covering the distance to the far shore. When
they were done, the battalion cooks made breakfast. "You ate it
outta your tin hat," my dad said.

At midday, the commanding general of the 2nd Armored
Division (nickname: "Hell on Wheels") was chauffeured onto
the bridge, stopping in the middle of the Rhine. He exited his
vehicle, raised the American flag, and posed for pictures.

"Then," my dad said, "he drove back off, and we proceeded to
reverse the process."

By midnight, the bridge was gone.

As his eighty-second birthday approached, Dad kept finding
new ways to stay busy. Once he'd learned of his diagnosis and
received his treatment schedule, he planned an ambitious backyard barbecue—which he dubbed the "Holy Smoker"—for early
June, giving himself something to look ahead to, a place to drive
his energy. For the second time in two years, he had a malignant
tumor inside of him, and this did not seem the central fact of
his life. Indeed, it seemed to be a benchmark against which his
actual life was being measured. He felt confident in the doctors'
prognosis and confident in his own resolve to take this all prag-
matically, a step at a time. A Cleveland Clinic team of doctors
known as the "tumor board" had conferred and determined that

he should be given the most rigorous treatment, that he could handle it, and that it offered the best prospects for a continued quality of life.

So he did not share my curious fascination with the seemingly fated, perhaps even allegorical, timing of everything: his five-day sequence of radiation treatments was to begin on my fiftieth birthday, a Monday, St. Patrick's Day.

He was far more interested in the party Gina threw for me the Saturday before.

He showed up in a green cardboard leprechaun hat, carrying a large heavy wrapped box, which he asked me to open early in the evening so it could be shared. He'd arranged with a local brewer to have a set of custom labels made for a case of "Davey O'Giffels Irish Stout." He had designed the labels himself on his computer, with a picture of me and script lettering above. They now adorned a dozen twenty-ounce brown bottles. I unwrapped the package, opened the first bottle, and poured us each a glass.

The house filled with people, and music, and the billowy smells of homemade pasta on the stovetop, and carry-out chicken, garlic and spice. Voices and laughter filled the downstairs. It was a big party in the way a big party is really a bunch of small parties all under the same roof. A gathering in the living room, another in the kitchen, one near the stereo, another in the smoky alcove outside the back door. Gina made sure everyone was overfed because it is her genetic belief that no one has ever had enough to eat. If acute restlessness is my family's disease, pathological hospitality is hers.

At the center of it all was my father, in his dopey green leprechaun hat. He joined in as a group of us raised our glasses to John. A friend invoked an Irish toast:

May those who love us, love us
And those who don't love us,
May God turn their hearts
And if He doesn't turn their hearts
May He turn their ankles
So we'll know them by their limping.

The party carried well into the early-morning hours of Sunday. The few of us who remained started digging deep in my record bins, and without irony or reservation, we blasted the Go-Gos, and Adam and the Ants, and Supertramp. The enduring image of that night, captured on a cell phone video, is of a friend whose name shall be stricken from the record, passed out flat on his back in my attic at four A.M., arms in crucifixion pose, an acoustic guitar lying across him, fingers in the death grip of an E chord at the top of the neck, the Cars' "Good Times Roll" playing at full volume two floors below, echoing through the room.

On Monday, my father received his first radiation treatment. He had to lie on his back, raise his arms above his head, hold his breath, and remain perfectly still while the technician aimed at the tumor, then blasted it with an intense dose of radiation.

That night, he came over for dinner. Said he felt fine. Normal.

On Tuesday, he returned to the clinic, received another nuclear blast to his chest, then went that night to a basketball game with my brother.

Thursday, he attended an event at the downtown library, where I was giving a reading to launch the release of my new book, which I'd dedicated to John. During the question and answer, a hand went up in the front row of the full auditorium. It was my dad.

"Your book is dedicated to John Puglia. Can you tell us why?"

Caught off guard, I gave my first response directly to him. "Really? You just did that?"

I took a long sip from my plastic water bottle, choked through the first words, then found my voice and explained as best I could this friendship that had defined so much of what was in the book I'd just read from. When my answer was finished, I scowled at him. "Thanks, Dad."

He smiled.

Friday, he returned for the fifth and final dose.

Saturday, I called and asked how he felt.

"I feel fine," he said almost quizzically. "Maybe a little tired. But not really."

18: BOB DYLAN'S BRAIN

"This coffin," Gina said one morning as we sat with coffee at the kitchen table, slowly dismembering the newspaper. "Where do you plan to store it?"

"I have an idea," I said.

I had no idea.

I had begun to do a thing I do, which is to deal with problems by diligently hoping they will go away on their own. Sometimes this works with plumbing. It often works with mild depression. It never works with property taxes.

As the box had slowly taken form, its physical and spiritual presence had taken on both size and shape that I hadn't entirely calculated. It was becoming real in the cosmic way people think of as "real" when they say things like "Shit just got *real.*" It's one thing to determine on paper that my resting corpse will be sixty-nine inches long and twenty-three inches wide at the coffin-pose elbow span. It's another to see and feel the wooden surface against which my postmortem self will rest.

This box was big. And it was heavy. And it wasn't even a box yet.

What it was still was a set of planks stacked against the back wall of my dad's workshop, with the graph-paper drawings taped to the front so we could refresh our memory whenever we returned to it. Since that day in late August when I'd left off on the sanding, life had repeatedly gotten in the way of the work to be done. Dad had retaken territorial rights to his workshop for his usual autumn process of building Christmas gifts. I'd been taken over by a busy semester and a book tour. Then he'd been taken over by the business of this lung tumor. And I'd been taken over by worrying about infringing on his time.

But one day in late winter, I stopped over to visit, and Dad suggested we go out to the barn and take a look. We trudged through the snow to the big red outbuilding, clomping our boots clean as we entered the doorway. The room beyond the glass door was warm and cinnamony with the smell of the wall-mounted gas heater. We hung our coats outside the workshop to keep them free of the dust that coated everything; even at its cleanest, the big room maintained its yellowy patina, the lingering toasted scent of cut wood.

The boards were resting where we'd left them. Their imperfections reintroduced themselves; their grains and cuts regained their distinction. I looked for the bloodstain but couldn't find it. We carried the boards to a set of sawhorses and laid them flat. Dad ran his hand along the surface, then knelt down to eyeball whether they'd warped or shrunk as they'd rested. "They look pretty true," he said. "Not bad."

For all the questions that had found their way into the process, I was reminded of why I had started the project in the first place. It was a way to spend time with my father. The year of his first go-round with cancer, I stood one day at my attic-office window. It was mid-November. I was looking out at a series of three backyard trees with wide, bright yellow leaves. Of the two dozen or so trees in my yard, these were the only ones that had not made their autumn release. It's like this every year: after all the other trees are bare, these three come bringing up the rear, a good fortnight behind, remaining green till they finally transition to the radiant color of Christopher Robin's raincoat. I'd never given it much thought, just figured that's the way things are.

A few days later, I was at my dad's house, and he was talking about raking his yard. "And of course I always have to wait on that one," he said, pointing to a big tree with those very same wide, bright yellow leaves. "Because it's a Norway maple, and they don't lose their leaves until a hard frost. Because, you know, they're from Norway."

An answer I hadn't asked for to a question I'd hardly realized was a question. He'd been teaching me like that his whole life, delivering knowledge, unprompted, in the natural course of our interactions.

I believed building my coffin could be a way to work through the bafflement of death. But the truth of my time alone with my father was that we were each finding ourselves too full of other parts of life for this to be an urgent and all-consuming venture. We were spending plenty of time together, in lots of ways. And plenty of time individually, each busy with life, enough so that scheduling what we sometimes called "coffin time" was often an infringement. Gina and I had begun having Dad over for dinner every Sunday, and this new ritual had become a highlight of the week. It seemed like the most valuable time we spent together was specifically the time not working on the coffin. In fact, Dad didn't want to assemble it permanently until we were both ready to put in a good chunk of continuous work to get it finished, because at that point it would occupy a lot of floor space in his workshop and would be in the way of anything else he wanted to accomplish there.

Meanwhile, I wasn't learning nearly as much from him as I'd expected. His design, based so much on his singular foresight and experience, had me at its mercy. It was like the workings of my automobile or Bob Dylan's brain: I didn't fully understand it, but I trusted it completely.

I'd believed that embarking on this scheme would allow me to learn some of the many skills and techniques of woodworking and design that I did not yet possess. In the ongoing renovation of our home, I'd become at least adequately proficient in certain skills—bricklaying, tree felling, floor sanding, drywall hanging, the inglorious unglunking of sewer lines. And I'd done some furniture building, but my main accomplishment in this field was decidedly crude—a set of rustic log furniture made from trees I'd cut down, stripping and curing the logs (all with my father's guidance), assembling the pieces in a free-jazz interpretation of traditional peg joinery, the final appearance of which had earned it a not entirely complimentary nickname from my friends: the *Gilligan's Island* furniture. I wanted to engage with advanced skills of fine carpentry, like those my father possessed. So far, my only significant progress was not losing fingers to a router mishap.

I'd believed that through our long hours in his workshop, I'd somehow absorb his life wisdom. The problem was—and I'd known this full well going in—my dad is not a bestowing-life-wisdom kind of guy. He's just not. And he never has been. One of the few times I went directly to him for Dad Advice—I was debating a high-risk career move—he listened silently to my whole spiel, sat for a long time deliberating, and finally declared that every time he took such a risk in his own professional life, it had worked out for the best. That was it: solid and unadorned, like the block lettering on his graph paper. It was the right advice, and it gave me the confidence I was seeking. But it's not the kind of thing that pours out of him naturally. (I, on the other hand, am more or less a Toys-R-Us water cannon of aphorisms and loose counsel with my own children, who I suspect think of me as a sort of emo mascot of the homestead.)

Maybe all my reasons were wrong.

The worst of these may have been the arrogance of believing I could understand death. The coffin wasn't helping much at all in this regard. I was still struggling to forgive my mother for her stubbornness near the end, her fatalism and abject refusal to follow any doctor's orders, her unwillingness (by my estimation) to eat properly, her passive insistence that all was in God's hands. I was only beginning to allow the fact that I couldn't know how much pain she was in. I was only beginning to acknowledge that she had a stronger faith than I did. In my selfishness, I took her death personally, as though it were something that had happened to me. I didn't want her to want to die because *I* didn't want her to die, because I still wanted the woman she had been to me, the woman with the deliriously infectious laugh, the woman who ate good food with such pleasure that it made one's lips move involuntarily in vicarious imitation, the woman who gave me *Nine Stories,* the woman at the crossword table thumbing through the OED. I hadn't allowed the possibility that her desire was an acceptance, maybe not much different than the acceptance my father had revealed, that he was at peace with the idea of dying, which struck me as healthy, maybe even noble.

And I certainly hadn't gained enough distance from the chaos of losing John to put that into order. The only progress I'd made there was the occasional sappy Facebook post about missing my friend, which in the world of Facebook is hardly a distinguishing emotion. Everyone on Facebook either loves their cat or misses someone who died. Trying to understand John's death just left me feeling inept and confused.

19: A DIVERSION

I did another thing I often do: I replaced what I was supposed to be doing with something else. This is the standard deduction of the workaholic.

On the afternoon of John's funeral the summer before, in the dense air under the white backyard canopy, I had sat talking with my friend Arnie Tunstall, the two of us perched at odd angles to each other in mismatched folding chairs. All around us, children ran, chasing one another this way and that through the backyard, throwing a basketball at the hoop, missing, throwing again, while the teenagers at their own table leaned forward eagerly in momentous conversation, and the adults, in pairs and threes and fours, sipped and talked at leisure.

Arnie had gone through art school with John, and like both of us, he had remained in Akron ever since. He had worked his way up the ranks at the Akron Art Museum, where he now managed the collections. We sat sipping cold beer and told old stories about John, laughing in that painfully odd way of funeral afternoons.

"We should do an exhibit," Arnie said.

"We could do a Dick Tappan retrospective," I said.

He laughed.

Our friend Andrew Borowiec joined us under the canopy. Andrew was a photographer and an art professor at the University of Akron, where he'd had John and Arnie as students. In the newspaper feature about John's life, Andrew had described him as having "more enthusiasm, curiosity and imagination than any student I've known in over 30 years of teaching." (In the twisted auto-translation, Andrew's assessment became "more enthusiasm, oddity and imagination than roughly any tyro I've famous in over 30 years of teaching.") Andrew had already begun the process of establishing a University of Akron scholarship in John's name. The fund would be used to send a student each year on the same field trip to New York that John had taken all those years ago, the one that, as much as anything, had established his aesthetic and his ambition, as well as his love for that city.

"We should," Andrew agreed when he heard the idea of an exhibit.

"It's what John would have done," I said.

Three months later, in October, I found myself in John's workspace, in the basement of the house where he'd thrown so many parties, the place where he'd put his life back together after his divorce, and the place where he'd died. John's family, sorting through his estate and at a loss to understand how to quantify all his artwork, had asked Arnie and Andrew to help catalog and give some sort of a monetary valuation to John's body of work. I'd joined them, along with another friend, Robbie Schneider, a coworker of John's who'd collaborated with him on work. Beyond the estate process, the four of us were hoping to get an idea of what work was available and what an exhibit might look like. John's parents and his younger brother, the executor of the estate, looked on, just hoping for some way to appraise this sprawling detritus of a busy mind.

This was strange work. At the exhibits the year before, paintings had sold for two hundred dollars. But John had also freely given pieces away. The snowy night of the Michael Dokes opening, Gina and I had bought one painting, and when the show came down, John had given us two more. In wide racks in his basement, we found a startling amount of work—John had been producing even more than I knew. Some was finished or nearly so. Some remained in early sketch form, some clearly marked with strokes of frustration, some apparently abandoned, giving way to a more polished version of the same idea. Many of the pieces were on the scale of those large vellum-and-ink pieces that had become his style in his last years.

I hadn't been down in John's workroom since the week he died, and being there now in his absence felt remarkably similar to the afternoon I'd found myself alone in my dad's workshop. All the effects of a man, the unstudied accumulation, the tumbledown trail of activity, the story a person leaves.

Hanging from a nail on the side of a shelf was the CBGB messenger bag he'd bought at the club's gallery eight years before. On his worktable was the bottle of Campari we'd sipped from one night down there, when he'd shown me some early factory paintings he was working on. A Barry Manilow poster from *Dynamite* magazine, Issue No. 43, 1977, hung on the lavatory wall across from a tattered and torn handmade flier for one of the few shows by the Generics, the garage band John sang in when we were eighteen and knew nothing but believed everything. And then there was the smell, the slightly musty carpet mingling with the scent of paper and ink, an underground smell. Most of the people who came to John's parties didn't know there was a bathroom in the basement, so I always used this one when I was there, to avoid the crowd. Leaving the din of the upstairs and entering this private place with its bluish shadows, where John busily maintained his own promise, was, oddly, among my favorite memories of those nights. I could hear his music bleeding in when I was down here, weird tangents of Americana and the underground—Granddaddy, Uncle Tupelo, the Mountain Goats, Modest Mouse.

Just about every guy I've ever known who has taken on a mortgage—that societal standard of adult responsibility—has immediately claimed a space within his new piece of real estate to be devoted specifically to the opposite of adult responsibility. I spent part of a summer helping my brother build a barn (the designer and principal builder of which was, of course, our father). The construction process itself was an indulgence in male pleasures: amateur masonry, beer drinking, uninhibited profanity, peeing from the rooftop. The final product extended those whims, as it sheltered a vintage tractor, a motorboat, and a drum kit.

This barn included a set of century-old rolling carriage-house doors that were the original garage doors from my house. I donated them to the barn, having replaced them with a roll-up door I'd scavenged from my dad's house when he'd converted half his garage into a laundry room. (These things are always circular in my family.) Once the barn was under roof, Dad designed a mounting system for the doors and toiled day after day while my brother was away at work, custom-fitting them and preparing the rollers and the opening. One rainy afternoon, he attempted to move a door leaned against the outside rear wall of the barn. It started to come backward on him, and in his attempt to get out of the way, he slipped in the mud and it came down on top of him, landing in such a way that he didn't take its full weight but was nonetheless trapped. Seventy-six years old, possibly injured, mud soaking thorough his clothes, he lay there thinking not that he was going to die but that he was going to be in big, big trouble with my mother, who frowned upon such self-inflicted misadventures despite their frequency. His cell phone was in his rear pocket, and he worked agonizingly to reach underneath his backside with his one free hand, but could not get the shoulder turned far enough to allow it. So he lay there some more, thinking. Then, slowly and carefully, he started wriggling in the mud, and he wriggled and pushed and wriggled and pushed, and after an hour or so, he managed to work himself out from under the door. Then he got right back to work. He figured he was already dirty, so why not? A new barn needs stories.

I've found that the best of these spaces are the imperfect ones, the ones unmeant for their purpose, claimed from a void of the unwanted. I'd built my first version back in my parents' basement, with those boards hauled from beside an alley Dumpster. John, as an adolescent, had taken over an old cellar pantry in his parents' home, where he set up his stereo and his meager but growing record collection (the Sweet, Devo, Monty Python's Flying Circus), along with his Super 8 equipment and the reels that represented his growing oeuvre—mostly stop-action animation involving plastic dinosaurs that inevitably were doused in gasoline and set afire, dying in the foul soup of their own flaming evil.

As soon as John and I each became homeowners, I took over the attic of my house and he took over the basement of his, and it was from these spaces that we continued the way we continued, the earnest mess of trying to be the selves we'd imagined we might become.

John's basement in that first house was poorly lit and poorly drained, and his work often smelled of old damp concrete and tree roots. When a crappy tavern up at the corner was torn down, John's "studio" temporarily inherited its rat problem. But if you can't make art with a watchful eye and a pellet gun at your side, you may just not be cut out for the work.

My space on the third floor, meanwhile, was unheated and un-air-conditioned. I typed away on my brand-new Brother "electronic" typewriter, which had a tiny display window above the keyboard allowing me to preview every seven words or so before the daisy wheel committed them to paper. In the winter, my longhaired literary self sat wrapped in a heavy parka and stocking cap, analyzing unfolding prose through the haze of my own breath. In the summer, I wrote shirtless, adhered by sweat to the turquoise vinyl backrest of the office chair I'd plucked from a curbside one garbage night.

The next place Gina and I moved to was the falling-down house we took on more or less as a lifelong shambolic immersion into our own permanence, chickens of which have been coming to roost ever since. I immediately claimed the squirrel-and-bat-infested third-floor servants' quarters, with broken windows and wisteria growing in across the floor, which Gina was more than happy to concede. John, meanwhile, slipped into a spell of instability as his marriage took a series of hairpin turns and spinouts that led him to one apartment, then another, then back into a shared home with his wife, then back out. (Sitting on his patio one night some years later, we tried to count the number of places he'd lived since moving out of his parents' house. He came up with seven. I came up with eight. I was right—he'd forgotten one.)

In each place, John had found a room of his own, and in each instance, he'd had to carve this space out of nothing. These are our most cherished spaces, the ones of our own making, the ones we have to force our way into. In order to create, we become uninvited aliens of storage rooms and crawl spaces, with bare bulbs above and plywood flooring below, and in so doing, we plant our little flags.

After Andrew and Arnie had finished the painstaking process of their inventory, we left John's house and reconvened at an old pub John had frequented, owned and bartended by a guy he had played Little League baseball with.

In the dim restaurant, we hashed out the idea of organizing an exhibit, a retrospective of John's work, to open on the first anniversary of his death, July 14, 2014. This gave us a goal and a deadline—nine months to get it together. Andrew suggested the University of Akron's art school gallery as a venue.

"There's a lot more of his work than I thought," Arnie said.

"There's way more than what's in his house," I said. "I think all of his friends have stuff. I know I do."

The gallery had two levels, and we came up with a plan for a two-part exhibit—one level featuring John's work, and the other filled with work by all the people he'd collaborated with, his other artist friends. We would also include an auction to raise money for the scholarship.

That night, on a scrap of paper, we began a list of things to do: contacting the gallery, determining an organizing principle for John's work, making a list of other artists to contact, people he'd published in his homemade magazines and included in gallery shows he'd curated. This community included people from all over the country, some of them famous—Mark Mothersbaugh and Gary Baseman—and some sort of famous—Cindy Greene, the singer for Fischerspooner; Aaron Burtch, the drummer for Granddaddy; and Dallas Wehrle, the bass player for the Constantines. John had a particular radar for musicians who made visual art, and they, it seemed, had a particular affinity for someone who recognized them this way.

We established some preliminary goals, set some deadlines, scheduled another meeting, and each of us got to work.

Meanwhile, my coffin sat dormant. It didn't have a deadline. It had to be finished before I died, but otherwise, its urgency was vague at best.

There was, however, the more pressing deadline of Dad's desire to regain control of his shop space. This was real. He continued to needle me about getting this thing finished and out of there. But until we glued it together into its box shape, it didn't take up all that much room.

And then the troubling deadline, the real one that always caused my brain to shut down: the ever lingering specter of my father's mortality. I was at a conference in Minneapolis, catching up with a writer friend over lunch, and I told him about the coffin project and how much time it was taking.

"David. What if, you know? I mean—he's in his eighties . . ."

"I know." I sighed. "Of course I've thought about it. I honestly don't know. I don't know what I do then."

And then came spring. I went out for a run one early evening and, without planning to, turned myself in the direction of John's house, which sat unsold. I cruised down the steep hill into the valley where he'd lived, and slowed as it came into view, a constellation of memories forming above me.

The "For Sale" sign was in the front yard, no car in the driveway. I wasn't sure if his sons were living there at that point. Everything had been in a state of uncertainty, and everyone involved just wanted the house to change hands cleanly and be done. I walked up the driveway to the patio and sat down in the chair where I'd sat the day I'd last found him here, fighting for air as he made his way across the small backyard. I sat there a long time, eyes closed and hands resting in my lap, aware that it might be the last time. My hands were folded in my lap and my head was tilted back and my eyes, closed, began to well up, but I was laughing. For everything else that lingered here, it was laughter that prevailed.

I sighed and spoke his name into the spring evening.

When I opened my eyes, I saw in the garden a small sculpture I'd given him as a Christmas gift several years before, made by a local junk artist, a steel plate, rusted brown, that vaguely invoked a barking coyote. I knew the house had been emptied of all of

John's personal items and was staged with furniture. I knew that
this piece had been forgotten. I grabbed it.

It weighed five pounds or so, which isn't much until you try
to run back uphill and around a sharp bend and uphill some
more, rusty steel banging against your thigh the whole way, a
mile and a half, working up a bruise, and that's when I knew
John was laughing for sure.

20: NEVER NOT WORKING

I woke up that morning, aware of the moment. Aware, really, of nothing else.

Three hundred sixty-five days before, I'd woken in this same spot and he was not quite yet gone. I lay in the cool sheets replaying a series of lasts—the last concert we attended together, the last drink we shared, the last time I made him smile, which was when I told him the parade in and out of his hospital room looked like an episode of *Pee-wee's Playhouse*.

The humid July morning carried distinct echoes of one year before, a morning when I woke up knowing that sometime very soon the phone was going to ring and that would be that. I'm sure there's proof that anniversaries are mathematically arbitrary, but I can't deny how uniquely and completely this day felt like the precise completion of a singular year.

Gina has always talked about the old-country tradition of formal mourning for a set period of time, the way her grandmother wore all black every day for a decade after her husband died, then returned to her usual wardrobe. That seems so clean and manageable. What I found was something more cyclical, something like the surf. The movement was forward and backward, forward and backward. There was progress, but it was not steady. It felt like I was traveling on a Mobius strip, never certain which side of the experience I was on.

But this day was a clear milestone, a definite step forward. Tonight we would be celebrating John with the opening of the exhibit. The response to our request for his friends to contribute had been overwhelming. Many of them had created new work to be auctioned at the show. Others had donated work that was worth hundreds, even thousands, of dollars. John's Italian-American family had taken the notion of the "reception" in the diligent manner of wedding planners; there would be tables set out with homemade pizzelles and cakes, pizzas and little sandwiches cut on diagonals. One of John's musician friends would be DJ-ing in the lobby. A lot of people would be coming.

I'd spent the previous afternoon helping hang the show in the gallery. When I arrived at the chaos of the half-finished exhibit, Arnie, the main curator, handed me a special museum cloth and cleaner and asked me to carefully wipe all the pieces now hanging on the white walls. I spent a couple of hours spritzing the cloth and wiping gently, the thickness of Plexiglas the only thing separating my fingers from the work of John's own hands. The large ink-on-vellum paintings, with their wavy, wrinkly texture, retained John's intimate interactions with his materials. Here, he'd lingered long enough for a bit of red ink to puddle. There, he'd barely brushed a stroke.

I'd been in his workshop countless times as these and other pieces were in process. John's inherent busyness had led to our collective choice for the title of the show: *Never Not Working*, from the Stein poem.

*   *   *

When I returned home that afternoon and signed in to my email, I was met with a *ding* and the still-active Outlook calendar reminder:

WALLY WAFFLE TIME
6 Days Overdue

I remembered our last breakfast together. I remember what he was wearing—a red-and-black-plaid western shirt with snap buttons, dark jeans, slate-gray high-top sneakers. He ordered an egg-white omelet and home fries but didn't finish. As we sat there, an old high school acquaintance happened by, a former athlete now dressed in a tracksuit, hair graying, the morning paper tucked under his arm.

"Hey, guys," he said. "Workin' hard or hardly workin'?"

We said hello, and he went off to read his paper, and we stared at each other for a long moment, sharing telepathic laughter.

"That's it," I said. "We have become old men."

The gallery was alive, kinetic, full of people and noise, constant motion. Arnie, having worked down to the wire, exhaled nervously as he straightened the framed exhibit poster hanging at the gallery entrance. There was so much pizza that we were already discussing who would take the leftovers to the homeless shelter at night's end. (A needless concern—we'd somehow failed to account for the appetites of the art students who would be drawn to the food table like sidewalk pigeons.) John's stylish cousin Rocco arrived in a pair of bright yellow pants—a man named Rocco in yellow pants!—and his parents arrived, and his sister and his brother and their families. John's sons, Sam and Jonathan, weaved throughout the crowd, young men carrying the halo of their boyhood despite the tattoos and the purposeful haircuts and the hint of smoke.

The first three pieces beyond the gallery entrance were old black-and-white portraits of John, prompted by a photography-class assignment given in this same building three decades before. Two had been made by fellow students who'd used him as a subject. The third was a self-portrait of the electric nineteen-year-old I admired and followed, blissful in an Adidas T-shirt, arms splayed, the sly smile, spray paint spattered intentionally across a corner of the mat. These images were shot on film, a medium that barely exists anymore, and in one way it gave the effect of history preserved, as though these frames had been captured by Mathew Brady at Antietam, and in another way, these images, so physical and handmade, tricked me to lift a finger to his blurred shoulder, as though I could reach across the divides of time and death and illusion. In one portrait taken by his class-mate, John was dressed in a Baja pullover that I remembered the instant I saw it, his thick hair threatening to burst into a full Afro, his big round glasses. The third portrait was of his face, life-size and closely framed, and although it was intentionally blurred for art-school effect, it also brought me the closest to who he was then, round and cheeky, so full of curiosity and big ideas and the fearlessness to pursue them. His eyes were soft and thoughtful, his lips full and relaxed, the slight tilt of his head peaceful and contemplative.

His face grew leaner as he grew older, less round as the last bit of baby fat drained away and his hairline receded and a little goa-tee extended his chin, and his eyeglasses became more angular, all his edges sharper. And then, in middle age, he filled back out, a combination of exercise and la dolce vita. After the first round of surgery and cancer treatments and the intense, deliberate life-style changes that followed, he grew lean yet again. Sometimes it seems like a lifetime occurs in a moment. And sometimes it seems to span eras upon eras, whole oceans of existence. With both John and my mother, the more I tried to calculate the true measure, the closer those two notions became until they were one, the way a flame consumes itself and twirls up into smoke, its essence and its absence.

The exhibit remained on display into the beginning of the fall semester. The director of the art school wanted students to see it, to know that this was the work of someone who had been just like them.

The fund-raising surpassed any of our expectations. Between the art auction and donations to the scholarship fund, over $12,500 was raised. The amount was enough for the scholarship to be self-sustaining. Eight months later, the first recipients of the John M. Puglia Endowed New York City Travel Fund for Art Students (an overwrought name that would have made him snicker and repeat the word "endowed") were honored at a student awards ceremony at the art school. John's family was there. Just up the stairs from the small auditorium was the janitor's room John had commandeered for his first big show back when he was a student, the factory installation that he'd staged there. It never returned to its original purpose. Three decades later, it was still being used for student exhibits.

As the closing reception approached, the local newspaper's

art critic scheduled a gallery tour with me and Andrew. We strolled with her through the big open rooms, providing background and context for John's work and the work of his friends. Her feature was the centerpiece story on the Sunday arts page. It included a line about John's publication, *M-80*, quoted directly from the press release I'd written: "The magazine featured images and writing by new and established local artists as well as nationally prominent artists, including Mark Mothersbaugh, Gary Baseman, Cindy Greene and Dick Tappan."

21: THE LONG HOME

The annual family Christmas gift exchange was really a yearly process of the four siblings idly trading restaurant gift certificates while waiting our turn for Dad to have our name. It's kind of like the NBA draft lottery. You have to be the loser for a few years to rise back up to the top. One's turn in the rotation meant receiving something from his workshop. The previous year, he'd presented me and Gina with a set of plans for a stone grotto he would build that summer alongside our patio. This year, he'd been working on a labor-intensive birdhouse for Ralph and his family, an insanely detailed replica of their actual house, with a barbecue grill and a toolshed attached to the sides, a garden trellis and tediously handmade window shutters. Working back through the years, he had bestowed us with a corner china cabinet, a buffet, a keepsake trunk whose lid was decorated with a sepia-tone photo of our first home. All of this came from his barn, as he spent every autumn working like the elf of Ohio, tinkering in his magic workshop. For many years, every stick of furniture Gina and I owned fell into one of three categories: 1) hand-me-downs; 2) curb finds; and 3) things made by my father. When we finally bought a proper dining room table, I believe he saw it as a challenge: within a few Christmases, he'd built the buffet and china cabinet to match it.

Meanwhile, it was our year to buy for my dad. He had dropped a not so subtle hint, an email stating he wanted either a half ton of No. 57 limestone driveway gravel or a "trim router—Porter Cable Model PCE6430 or DEWALT Model DWE6000." Which meant he wanted the trim router. I began researching.

My dad already owned a nice high-end router. He had a full bench setup. This tool he'd requested was described in the online literature as a single-speed laminate trimmer, which didn't clear it up for me in the least. Isn't a router a router? And what sort of laminate work did he have in mind? Nevertheless, it was right in the meat of our usual agreed-upon spending limit, about a hundred dollars. So I drove out to the home improvement superstore, bought the DeWalt model DWE6000, and wrapped it up for our Christmas Eve gathering.

We all convened at my brother Ralph's house for a family dinner and, afterward, began the paper-strewn anarchy of gift-exchanging. My dad smiled when I presented him the compact, heavy rectangular box. He held it before him, testing its weight. "Bourbon?" he asked, pretending to raise it to his lips before tearing open the wrapping. Then, upon seeing the box, he declared, "Where's an outlet? Let's fire it up."

I arrived the day after Christmas. I had to let myself in because he couldn't hear me knocking over the whine of the shop vacuum. The first order of business was to clean up his workshop, which had fallen into a chaos of clutter and sawdust. He shut down the vacuum when he saw me.

"Howdy," I said, scanning the room, trying to determine which part had been cleaned and which had yet to be. I didn't want to hurt his feelings by asking. I set my coffee thermos on the tool-strewn workbench, across from the yellow-and-black router box, still unopened. "What do you want me to do?"

"Anything. Take your pick. Here," he said, grabbing a cardboard box by its flap and handing it toward me. "You can gather up all the loose lumber scraps."

He fired the vacuum back up and I got to work, picking up cutoffs and half-boards from the debris field around the table saw. Slowly, over the course of an hour or two, with him working one end of the room and me working the other, a sense of order started to return. I swept one large corner clean, brushed the dust from the top of the router bench, pulled the heavy four-legged contraption into the clean spot, then swept the area where the bench had been. Cleaning a workshop is always a tedious box-step. You clear one area, move everything into that part of the floor, clean the place where it was, move it back, until things begin to settle into where they belong.

I took over the vacuum while my dad worked on gathering up his scattered tools and hanging them back where they belonged. As I dragged the vacuum's tube slowly back and forth across the floor, it left stripes, alternating gray concrete with fine sticky yellow dust. After vacuuming the floor and all the tabletops, I began working on the walls, which were fouled with a combination of sawdust and cobwebs that hung there like twine. I made my way to the back of the room, where the pieces of the coffin remained, old plans still taped to the front, untouched for sixteen months as life had continued to be in the way.

By midafternoon, the place was as clean as a workshop ever

gets. It smelled of mellow sawdust and the yellowy tang from the gas heater and a lingering syrup of linseed oil. The room was warm from the heater and the activity, bright under the fluorescent lights.

We stood for a moment facing into the space, unsure whether we were finished or ready to begin.

"Well?" he said. "It's early. Should we see if these pieces still fit together?"

"Okay. Let's do it."

We went to the back of the room, where the big planks leaned one against the other. We had to do some remembering. He pulled loose the sheet of graph paper taped to the front board and smoothed it on the flat metal top of his band saw. He had to turn it upside down a couple of times to remember which way the design was supposed to face. Once he did, he began to explain how one piece would overlap another to build out the trim, tracing a craggy yellow fingernail along the graph paper. He paused on a particular detail. "Wait—is that the way we're supposed to go?"

"Dad," I said. "You lost me five minutes ago."

"Well, that makes it easy," he responded. "Let's just deal with the big stuff and worry about the details later."

I carried a set of sawhorses into the workshop from where they were stored in the barn's outer room. Together, we laid the plywood bottom across their span. Then we brought over the sides and the ends. We'd made a series of markings on them to show which edges matched up. But that was a long time ago, over a year, and now they looked like some other culture's hieroglyphs.

Flipping and rotating the boards, we eventually arranged the pieces how we thought they were supposed to go. We folded the various boards up into the shape of a box. When everything was in place, we stood there, facing each other, each with our arms embracing an end, its shape requiring all four of our hands and elbows. If we let go, it would all tumble apart. If one of us lost his grip, the other would have to compensate. But there, with everything in balance, the box revealed itself: a long open space between us.

There's an ancient term for the grave: "the long home." It appears in the Bible, in Ecclesiastes: "and the almond tree shall flourish, and the grasshopper shall be a burden, and desire shall fail: because man goeth to his long home, and the mourners go about the streets."

And desire shall fail. I wonder maybe if that's what death really is. The end of wanting.

So now this box was a clumsy wooden thing between me and my dad that couldn't stand without us. A long home. The scent of dust; a shared labor; a warm room. And a trust—more than anything else, at least for now, a trust that there was some purpose in this, and that one or the other or maybe both of us would come to its truth.

We looked at each other and chuckled at our conundrum. We were kind of trapped. Neither of us could let go.

"Now what?" I said.

"Slide your hands forward and squeeze the sides tight," he said after a long consideration. "I'll put some clamps on it to hold it together."

I stood with my arms trapping the pale blond wood together, pressing hard toward the center. My dad grabbed a small armload of the longer furniture clamps and began to set them. "You can let go now," he said. I stepped back and looked at it. He was at my side. "It's starting to look like something," he said.

"It is," I said.

It was big. It was bigger than I imagined it would be. Deeper. For some reason, that was my main impression: that if I were inside, I would be lost in its depth. I had a fleeting image of drowning, that somehow if I were inside and my head passed below the surface of the opening, I would be swallowed up.

"What should we do now?" I said.

"No turning back. Next step is to put it all together. But I'm out of glue. And we're gonna need a lot."

"I guess we just walk away from it for now."

"Yep. Stop on your way home and pick up two big bottles."

I grabbed my thermos and pushed open the heavy glass-paneled door, pulling my coat from where it hung on the hook just outside.

"Get the good stuff," my dad said. "We don't need the bottom dropping out of this thing."

I have a theory that I'm sure is true. The only reason humans continue to explore new horizons is as an excuse to purchase new tools. I suspect that Lewis and Clark set off for the American West primarily because it would allow them to buy cool new spyglasses and hiking staffs. Space exploration has always, to me, seemed secondary in the NASA mission, with the real purpose being the development of badass hardware and innovative methods of defying gravity and ingenious systems to deliver liquefied hamburgers to the digestive system. Anyone who was an eight-year-old boy witnessing the *Apollo 15* moon buggy's debut knows damn well exactly what was going on. A high-level government scientist had just built a space dragster.

At the same time my dad and I were assembling the box,

my city's mayor was making a bold proposition. Faced with the daunting necessity of a $1.4 billion sewer overhaul project, he proposed that the city start its own construction company to boost local employment. As a way to kick-start this, he set out to purchase six concrete trucks and four dump trucks. The plan failed, but I totally got it. After all, I had once come dangerously close to buying a dump truck myself.

It was only a matter of time before the truth of my dad's Christmas request revealed itself. He'd designed the corners of the box as rabbet joints, with the mitered ends intentionally left long, so after they were joined, they could be trimmed precisely and sanded smooth and flush. We had finally glued the four sides together, forming a frame, still with no bottom. Now that the box was assembled, those long rabbet ends stuck out about a quarter inch. As I ran my thumb down one of these, I asked how we were going to cut off the excess.

"That's what the trim router is for," my father said.

Now I understood. This hundred-dollar specialty tool had been acquired for a single step in my project.

He went to his workbench and opened the top of the yellow cardboard box, removing the router and the accessories in their clear plastic packaging. Setting the instructions aside, he turned the router upside down and figured out how to open the chuck. Then he went over to one of the dusty shelves on the wall and pulled out the old wooden bourbon box where he stored his router bits. He found the one he wanted, tightened it into the chuck, then clicked the switch.

Whhhhzzzzzzzzz!

The tool whined in a pleasing oscillation of speed and power. Gripping its small casing with one hand, Dad approached the nearest corner of the box, set his feet in position, lowered himself slightly so his eyes were level with the corner, and eased the router's guide plate along the edge of the box. Cautiously, he worked the spinning bit into the overlap of pine. A plume of rough sawdust flew upward, and the air filled with the piping howl of sharp steel chewing wood. He moved the tool upward, slowly and sure-handedly, as I stood watching.

"Nothing like having the right tool," he called above the high tenor of the spinning steel. He grinned.

When he had finished several passes with the router, he shut off the switch and waited till the blade stopped spinning.

"Wanna try?" he offered.

"I thought you'd never ask," I said.

"Take it slow," he warned. "And make sure you've got the guide tight against the end. If it starts to roll, you'll ruin the corner."

I thumbed the switch and felt the torque take its own control. Holding the tool with both hands, I tentatively maneuvered it into place, then inched it into its first cut. Hot dust spewed from the hole at the center of the clear plastic guide, and after six inches or so, I began to feel my confidence. I adjusted my stance, finding the balance between me and this tool, its thrilling newness. My dad stood back near the door, overseeing. I glanced at him. He nodded. I kept going. At one point, I pushed too hard and the bit protested, whinnying. I eased back on the pressure. The router settled back in.

When I was finished, I turned off the switch and ran my thumb along the newly planed edge. Satisfied, I looked up at my father, wondering if he was ready for another turn. His arms were folded. He gestured with one hand.

"It's your coffin. Keep going."

22: MARKING TIME

My first time inside my coffin was not exactly what I'd imagined.

I was squatting on the cold concrete floor of the workshop, craning my neck into the unfinished wooden box, which was resting upside down on sawhorses. I'd been firing the nail gun from above into the plywood bottom, attaching it to the frame, and had missed the mark with a few of the nails, leaving them protruding through the plywood. I'd crawled underneath with a nail puller and was extracting the errant shanks. As morbid as assembling one's own casket might seem, more morbid yet would be to lie down in it one day on a bed of one's own sloppily driven nails.

As I squinted up into the darkened pine-scented interior, head and shoulders fully enclosed, my dad continued working outside. Each firing of a nail *KA-CHUNK!* into the wood was compressed *KA-CHUNK!* and amplified, a dense *KA-CHUNK!* concussion that caused me to recoil, worrying with each *KA-CHUNK!* that I'd be shot dead should a nail pierce through the three-quarter-inch plywood, enter my skull, and send me to the most ironic death imaginable. One of my long-standing goals is not to die an ironic death.

About that plywood. As with everything thing else having to do with wood choice on this project, my father had insisted we needed to buy a pressure-treated sheet, the chemical-greenish lumber intended to inhibit termites and decay and so forth. I had reminded him again that decomposition was an unavoidable consequence, and there was little benefit to its delay. Also, the pressure-treated was more expensive. I'd bought a regular sheet.

It wasn't until I was fully engaged in the work of nail pulling, feeling like I was being carpet-bombed from above by a nail gun, that it occurred to me: I was indeed inside my casket for the first time. I'd caught it—and myself—unaware, entering from below, before it was ready. I liked it. It felt close and intimate. Warmer than the rest of the room. It smelled good. I didn't even mind the sound now that I'd gotten used to it. I love rock and roll enough to appreciate good amplification and tone, and this box had the profound resonance of an AC/DC drum riff.

When I finally emerged, lying on my stomach and shinny-ing out from underneath, I made the announcement to my dad. "Well, that's it," I said above the continuing thrum of the air compressor, brushing sawdust from my shirtfront. "I have been inside my coffin."

"Yeah? How'd you like it in there?"

"Loud," I said.

"Enough to wake the dead?"

"Something like that."

The bottom was attached. When we'd finished cleaning up the bits of excess glue that had squeezed out of the joints, we eased the coffin off the sawhorses and stood it on end. I stepped back and looked at it. And what I saw standing vertically there was not a casket. What I saw, suddenly and unexpectedly, was a bookcase. A very heavy, decently proportioned, overbuilt, and baroquely conceived bookcase.

I made a quick calculation. Shelves could be mounted in a way that they could be removed later, with only small holes where the brackets had been. And those holes could be filled, or they could be left as part of the story. And those shelves could hold anything, for as long as I was alive.

"Dad," I said. "I think I've just found an elegant solution."

Winter got hardcore serious. The snow mounds in the driveway grew and grew, and they never melted. Usually, Ohio experiences a spasmodic freeze-thaw cycle that leaves a profound abundance of potholes. But this winter had been uniformly arctic. As with everything else about the challenges of living in northern Ohio, I relished the fight and rose to it. I am a meticulous shoveler—no snowblower for me!—and by late January, the sculpted walls of snow lining the edges of my long driveway were likely visible from the International Space Station. The white architecture was a proud achievement, and I protested with undue harshness when my new-driver daughter backed into one of the snow walls and left a big bumper divot. There were days when the snow was incessant, and I'd shovel two or three times between dawn and dark and sometimes beyond just to keep ahead. I'd maintained a shoveled path to allow the dog to go out, the rest of the backyard being too deep for her short beagle legs. By February, that opening looked like a stage-set passageway for the *Ice Capades,* if the *Ice Capades* included a circle of poop.

Another semester had begun, and the visits to my dad's barn tailed off. I made a few treks out there over the course of the continuing winter, my boots squeaking on the narrow snowblower path he'd maintained from the house to the barn, and we accomplished some small steps of progress, but as before, the flurry of activity during my break from school gave way to more pressing concerns. My dad always had plenty to keep him busy.

I missed our time together in the shop, but he continued coming over every Sunday for dinner. I had friends whose aging parents had become a burden in one way or another—emotional, financial, physical. I knew lots of people who'd been through the hell of Alzheimer's. I think the most difficult challenge has to be the parent whose demeanor changes radically, either through disease or the increasing crankiness that accompanies the discomfort of age or whatever the decline of life entails, a grinding down of the old charisma, so that an adult child finds himself visiting with the person he has known longer than anyone else, but it is no longer the same person. This happened with my mother in her later years, when her carefree, adventurous spirit gave way to the pain of her body and the rising force of her mortality, and conversations with her narrowed themselves into the subjects of her health and her discomfort. She was still generous with her love, but these moments came as less frequent counterpoints to her dark and quiet distress.

My dad, though, had remained good and welcome company. He had season tickets with my brother Louis to the University of Akron football and basketball games, and dinner invitations that filled his weekends and many of his weeknights. My brothers and our dad and I began attending monthly beer-tasting dinners at a favorite local restaurant, and very quickly, our father became the unofficial mascot of these events, always greeted with particular cheer by the chef and owner, who had nicknamed him

"The Monsignor" and doted on him, keeping his glass full. I realized that winter that I was spending more time with my eighty-two-year-old father, and in the same kinds of social pursuits, than I had been spending with John in the final years of our life together. And often my dad had more stamina than I did. Some Sundays, as he and Gina and I and our daughter, Lia, sat in a foursquare euchre arrangement, I, a person who had always taken pride in my own endurance, was the one to declare that this would be the last round, otherwise he might keep us all up well past midnight.

One Sunday, I invited him to come over early. The Richard Linklater film *Boyhood* had just been released on DVD, and I'd borrowed a friend's copy. The movie had intrigued me for the same reasons it intrigued a lot of people, filmed in annual sessions over the course of twelve years, as a boy (both the actor, Ellar Coltrane, and his character, Mason Evans, Jr.) grows up in real time on the screen, along with his family, from ages six to eighteen. But it also intrigued me for more distinctly personal reasons. Ellar/Mason was just a year younger than my son, Evan, and the main focus of the film was his relationship with his father; father/son relationships were a consuming fascination of mine for increasingly complex reasons. This film fed straight into my appetite for high-concept narrative, and I intended to add a meta-wrinkle by placing my own three generations of men together on the couch to watch it.

This, of course, failed. For one thing, the movie was long and slow-developing, yet I had created a situation in which neither my dad nor Evan felt like they could just watch idly, or wander off if they wanted to. I, an emotive person, had essentially made hostages of two patently nonemotive people—a civil engineer who came of age under Eisenhower and a self-conscious teen-ager who himself had not yet fully come of age. We sat in a row on the sofa, knee to knee in the darkened living room, staring at the screen. Slowly, everyone aged.

I don't think either of them disliked the movie, necessarily. Evan responded more than once with mild glee at recognitions that he'd been the same age when a certain bit of pop culture—Game Boy Advance SP, Soulja Boy—would intersect with Mason's life. When, after nearly three hours, the credits finally rolled, Dad set his palms on his knees, stood up, stretched, and announced that it was time for Manhattans, and we reverted to our usual unstudied chairs in the kitchen, where Gina was cooking some-thing that smelled delicious.

Date: 2/24/15
Subject: Cleve Clinic
From: [dad]

Had my 9 month follow up today. 3 Things:

1. The chronic cough is related to the treatment. The developing scar tissue is somehow interfering with the left lung air passage. He gave me some strong cough medication for temp. relief and some mild steroid treatments to alleviate it. This is nature's cure method. If this doesn't work, there is a procedure to correct which is last resort.
2. The CT Scan shows that the tumor is shrunk with no signs of life. Like spraying a wasp with wasp spray.

3. CT Scan also revealed a new tumor in right lung, small but capable of growth. There may be other new, tiny tumors lurking and he wants to identify and treat the whole. He is scheduling a PT Scan for next week. Nothing here I haven't been through before. I'll give more detail when I have time. Right now I'm going to eat my Swenson's Galley Boy and choc milkshake and head to the St. V game.

This email represented a confusing bit of déjà vu, a lung tumor diagnosis coming exactly a year after the previous lung tumor diagnosis. It all blurred together—the diagnosis, the treatment options, the decision to undergo a week of daily radiation blasts, and the way these things kept happening on the anniversaries of other things, so that the years were beginning to line up, for me, as benchmarks of disease and dying. I found myself again running math through my head, trying to put things in order.

2011: John and Dad, cancer.
2012: John and Dad, better; Mom died.
2013: John died; Dad new cancer, left lung.
2014: Dad, better; no one died.
2015: Dad, new cancer, right lung.

This logic process was beginning to resemble the bookshelves in my office. My books are arranged chronologically in the order I read them, and I almost rabidly maintain them in this order. Whenever they've been moved, I've meticulously replaced them in sequence, afraid of the consequences if that were lost. The importance has only grown as time—and the corresponding number of spines on the shelves—has gone on.

I can touch any spine in that collection and immediately recall exactly where and when I read that book. If I were asked, I couldn't tell you, for instance, what year we visited Virginia for a family wedding. I'm pretty sure it was 1997. Except I know I read T. C. Boyle's *Riven Rock* during the car trip, and as I approach the shelf now, I can hone in on the tangible chronology and declare with surgical precision that it was December 1998. These books don't just keep a time line. Their bindings and pages trace a narrative of who I was at every step along the path of my life. They tell me who I am by way of where I have been.

In the same way, the confounding blur of illness and suffering and death of the past several years regains a linear coherence through the chronology of cancer: Mom's throat, John's esophagus, Dad's throat, John's lungs, Dad's left lung, Dad's right lung, etc. These are the markers by which I identify when other events occurred. But that linear coherence is indeed shot through with other life events not connected to death and disease. Even as my dad's new diagnosis represented a new volume in this collection, a greater balance was continuing to form for me, with other, brighter events holding their space along the time line. Dad's lung tumor, for instance, coincided with the celebration of John's memorial exhibit; John's decline accompanied Evan's symbolic passage into manhood.

"In three words," says Robert Frost, "I can sum up everything I've learned about life: It goes on."

As soon as Dad had determined when his week of treatment would occur, he strategically scheduled Holy Smoker II, giving him a date in June to aim for.

He underwent the treatments. At his follow-up meeting a few weeks later, his doctor declared, "You have a lot less cancer than you did when I met you."

23: THE COFFIN PROBLEM

There was no way around it. My coffin had become a pain in the ass. We hadn't worked on it for months, and in the meantime it had represented nothing but a large, immobile obstacle in the middle of the dusty workshop where Dad continued to produce.

In those long months, he built Ralph's Christmas gift.

He built a series of cedar birdhouses with carved comical faces that he donated to charity auctions.

He built a decorative shelf to display beer steins behind Louis's bar.

He built another shelf to display a train set, also for the bar.

As a gift for one of his nieces, he turned an old walnut post into a garden pedestal, crafting an octagonal top from various pieces of exotic wood (the same pieces I'd coveted and been denied).

He built a pergola for a garage, an entrance ramp for a barn, a set of basement stairs. He reframed a door at my sister's house, helped me repair a burst water pipe, and continued the ongoing upkeep of his own house and yard.

*　　*　　*

I woke up one morning after a middle-of-the-night bout of insomnia, during which my imagination had conjured up a strangely destructive reverie.

"I had a sort of waking dream last night," I said to Gina as we stood in our pajamas on opposite sides of the bed, hair disheveled, pulling the sheet taut and smoothing it between us.

"What was it?" she said, dropping a pillow into place.

"A potential solution to end this whole coffin problem." I hadn't told her yet of my idea to turn the box into a shelf, worried she might reject the plan and I'd be back to having no idea what to do with it until my death.

"What?" she said, straightening the comforter. "Suicide?"

I dropped my pillow and scowled. "Um, no? No, my idea was to rip the whole thing apart, sort of like performance art, like that Art of Noise video where they destroy the piano. And then I could use the wood for something else."

"Oh," she said. "I was just thinking, you know, your unexpected death would be kind of an interesting plot twist."

"And then you wouldn't have to store it."

"And I wouldn't have to store it."

"You're weird sometimes."

"I'm not the one who's building a coffin."

This was, unfortunately, not the first time I'd found myself with a coffin problem. A number of years before, I'd had the opportunity to obtain an abandoned 1977 MG Midget for the cost of a salvage title and towing fee. It then sat in our garage for five years. I was in no position of insight. I just knew that the idea of owning a little British roadster was brilliant, and the idea of getting it practically for free made me a sort of hero. I'd managed to get the Midget engine to turn over once or twice with strenuous hand cranking, but it never caught. Nevertheless, it maintained its air of promise, as I dreamed of buffing its grimy sun-faded maroon exterior to full gloss, of hearing the putter of my own success under the hood. Eventually, I gave up and sold it for a hundred bucks.

This was followed by a full set of distressed wicker furniture I greedily plucked from a curb one night and carried down into my basement, where it then occupied a preciously large percentage of my workshop space for more years than I care to remember, awaiting my healing touch. I'd checked out a book from the library on how to wind wicker—this furniture was "distressed" in near-fatal ways—and I had calculated that I could teach myself the craft of upholstery and that one day this free set of furniture would reign as the centerpiece of a patio, which I would also have to build. Eventually, I abandoned this plan and set the furniture out on my own curb, where it was quickly plucked by another greedy salvage picker. God bless him (or her).

This was followed by an excited phone call from my father one day, telling me that he was at a construction site where thousands of old red street-paving bricks had been dumped and would be plowed underground unless someone wanted to haul them away, which led to a frantic making of arrangements—this was the moment when I seriously considered buying a dump truck, ownership of which would have represented a coffin problem of its own—and then the daunting presence of a huge mound of red paving bricks in my backyard and a phone call back to my dad asking how to design a driveway.

My mother was as complicit as my dad. She had passed down the gene of hopeless imagination and an instinct for bringing impractical whims to fruition. When she decided that my dad needed a parrot (this was a completely one-sided conclusion), she found one at a pet store, somehow kept it hidden in the White Bedroom for two weeks, and presented it as his Christmas gift. So now my dad had a pet parrot, entirely as a result of my mother's belief in her ability to corral the improbable. (There was also the contributing factor of my father's high tolerance for absurdity.)

"Corral" is an operative word here. Mr. Blifel, the parrot, was not even the most improbable animal to occupy the old family home. There was a long history in that house of unconventional pets that had arrived under unconventional circumstances. One Easter, my parents gave each of us a baby chick, which itself was not that unusual among Catholic families at the time, but I never knew any other kids who got to keep theirs to maturity. We did. Mine was a rooster.

The next year, we got a duck. We named it Waddle. This might seem like an awfully pedestrian name for a duck in a household that also included my mother, the Namer of Things, but the duck was not named simply for its gait. It was named after Dave Wottle, a local-native-turned-Olympic-gold-medal runner whose gimmick was wearing a billed cap. Waddle/Wottle grew quickly through the spring and summer, chasing us around the backyard and nipping with its orange plastic lips at our fingers and pant legs. When the weather turned cool, my dad built a pen in the basement, but there were territory issues between the duck and Bette Davis Eyes, so our pet soon was transferred to a local nursing home with a reflecting pond.

Finally, one Easter, my mother went for broke in terms of religious symbolism, sauntering into the living room with a young lamb on a leash. We kept "Ali Baba" all summer. She grew large, with the carriage and musk of livestock. My kid brother rode her like a pony, and the four of us took her for walks through the neighborhood on a leash. My parents said if we were ever stopped by a policeman, we were to say it was our sheepdog. I think this was a joke, but what did I know?

By autumn, it was clear Ali needed to go, and my parents contacted a sheep farmer who promised to take her as a pet, under the assurance that she would not be butchered. He arrived in an old sedan with his wife and a daughter who looked to be my age and seemed a little . . . off, an impression half-explained when the farmer mentioned that she'd been butted by a sheep when she was young and had suffered some sort of damage. They returned to the car, the farmer and his wife settling into the front seat after loading our sheep into the back with the daughter, the one who'd been attacked by a sheep.

My mother's impulsiveness meant that she didn't know anything about the bird she had purchased other than that it was a parrot. In fact, it was an orange-winged Amazon, captured in the wild. They are loud and dirty and mean. And they have a life expectancy of up to a hundred years. Which meant that even now, well after she was gone, my dad was still in charge of the daily care and feeding of her long-ago caprice.

24: FURNITURE OF SORTS

As a new year began, my dad and I found more time to work. The lid of the coffin would be a stacked series of four rectangular oak frames that formed a low-profile pyramid. The process was technically demanding. Each of the layers required miter cutting and fitting 45-degree corners. We were making the cuts with my brother's electric chop saw, whose big round blade made cutting far easier than did my dad's hand-operated miter saw. But it was impossible to get the four corners all to meet cleanly.

"This is a great tool," my dad said as we leaned in together, eyeballing a joint with a frustrating eighth-inch gap at its corner. "But it's for building houses, not making furniture."

To hide the imperfections of our work, he had come up with a plan to inset oak splines across the corners. Each spline required the painstaking setup of a jig to guide the router, using a series of clamps—fifteen or more—to hold everything in place. At last, when everything was right, my dad would pull the router forward, one pass only, steady as she goes, a plume of mealy yellow dust spewing out like sand from a dune-buggy tire. Twenty-four times we did this.

Three days into our new routine, I'd warmed back up to the process. Long into the evening, I could still taste the chewy air of the workshop, its toasted nutmeg lingering in that singular space where scent meets imagination. As I left the barn each afternoon, exiting into the winter chill, little problems persisted in my mind. I awoke in the middle of the night after the third consecutive day of work, thinking about how each layer of the lid would fit, with the final piece as a sort of capstone. I thought of my mom's hundreds of rosaries. What if I removed the crucifix from one of them and inset it into the lid? This is something John would have thought of, I mused, something decorative and ritualistic. But it wasn't John's idea, and it wasn't my dad's. It was small, but it was mine.

This corner was particularly obstinate. The 45-degree cut wasn't clean—my fault—with a slight but unacceptable convex. We tried a second cut, we sanded and shimmed, but the two boards refused to meet on a level plane. I stood on one side. My dad stood on the other. We stared at it, frustrated.

"What if I put extra pressure on top of the router while you pull it through?" I suggested. I leaned across to his side of the table and placed my crossed palms atop the yellow router casing. "Like this. And then I'll push down while you pull."

He nodded. "That could work. I don't know any other way."

He started the motor. I set my hands on top, and slowly, we eased into the cut. After an inch or so, I felt the router depress beneath the pressure of my hands, as though I were pushing suddenly into cookie batter.

"Stop!" my dad groaned, fumbling for the switch. "We ruined it," he said before the motor was even done winding down.

We hadn't accounted for the fact that I was pushing down

on the portion of the tool not locked into place. My pressure had caused the router bit to drill past the quarter-inch set and through the opposite side of the boards.

We stared at it a long moment. I'd pushed a hole right through the lid.

"Can we hide it with a spline?" I asked.

Splines had become our magic solution. But this was a stretch.

"Maybe. If we're lucky. I don't know."

"Even if not," I said, "the bad part will be on the inside of the lid."

"Think about that," my father said. "People are going to spend more time seeing the inside of the lid than the outside."

"Including me," I said.

I returned for another day of work. The time away had allowed each of us to refine our reaction to the damage I'd caused.

After a spell of assessment and discussion, we carefully cut and fitted a strip of wood into the groove we'd routed. It worked. We were able to hide the ragged hole.

As we began setting up to rout out yet another corner, Dad mentioned that his electric bill had arrived in the mail. Three hundred dollars.

"It's all this," he said, referring to the power tools and dust collection motor. "It really sucks it down."

I'd been keeping a tally of the costs, saving receipts for everything. But those were just my expenditures. I hadn't calculated his contributions—electricity, wear and tear on his tools, glue and screws and nails. And certainly not his labor. A corollary to the genetic restlessness of my dad and brothers is that we consider our work to be an economic advantage. If I can spend a weekend cutting down a tree and splitting the logs, I've saved the cost of both a tree service and a cord of firewood, and in my mind, that's the same as making money. Nevertheless, he was putting a lot into this coffin that wouldn't show up in my accounting.

Work continued on the lid. As my father set up the router to put a scrolled edge on the corners of the stacked layers of boards, I clamped one of the frames to a set of sawhorses. Dad did a test run on a scrap piece of lumber, checked it, and nodded approvingly. He handed the router to me. "Here. You do it."

I accepted the tool. Dad stepped back to watch. I eased tentatively into the first run along the edge.

"Don't take too much in one pass," he said. "Just keep going over it. A little more each time. Be patient. And don't let it tilt on you. Keep flush to the board."

Slowly, I started to get a feel, recognizing in the whine of steel chewing through oak how deep I was cutting. The work took a lot of physical effort and control as I held tight to the two molded black handles. The machine spit a constant stream of hot sawdust into my face; I could feel it filtering down into my flannel shirt. After the first edge was done, I shut off the motor, shook out my shirttail, wiped my glasses clean, and brushed off my stocking cap. Then I ran another edge. All the while, Dad watched, arms folded, leaning against the door.

I changed router bits and went to work on the inside edges, a different feel, a different grain. I'd been at it for two hours and felt like I'd been waterskiing through wood pulp, my sinuses clogged with dust, chest itching from the oak tendrils, forearms tight, jaws clenched, eyes irritated, and lenses clouded.

When the routing was finished, we assembled the lid temporarily atop the casket's opening. Dad pulled the cap piece from the sawhorses and set it in place. He laid his palm against it and leaned down, eyeballing the lines.

He stepped back, still keeping his eyes affixed to the box. He chuckled. "You know what? This looks pretty good."

I'd been wiping my eyeglasses on my shirttail. I replaced them and stepped back. Unexpectedly, it looked different. It looked complete. It looked elegant. It looked like furniture.

25: A DISTINCT
LACK OF SHALLOWNESS

"I think you've got a problem," Paul Hummel said, extending the tape measure upward for a third time.

He stood in the bright fluorescent light of my father's workshop, a swipe of sawdust on the sleeve of his navy blazer, another on his crisp gray dress slacks, his blue eyes staring down at the casket, which rested on a set of sawhorses with its lid set temporarily on top.

"It's too tall. It won't fit in the vault."

I thought he was joking. In under five minutes since his arrival, he'd already asked if we'd tricked out the inside of the lid with a Kindle, and suggested we turn the box on its side and use it to hold pony kegs, and pondered the temperature it would reach if we fed it into his crematory. Undertaker humor: his stock-in-trade. I figured this was just him continuing to yank our chains.

But then I looked at my dad, and he wasn't smiling. He was already calculating something I was slower to grasp. The process of evolution on the lid, adding the tiered layers, which now, finished, looked classically composed and which Paul himself had initially described as beautiful, had also lured us away from our adherence to the measurements I'd scribbled in a notebook four years before, when I had toured the funeral home's casket room with Paul as my guide.

I'd invited him here to see it, hoping to get his opinion of the work and, as my email had said in jest, "see if we've made any grievous errors." He'd made time between appointments to stop by. His first reaction had been encouraging. He paused just inside the old beveled-glass door and took it in with admiration, chuckling in approval. "That is *really* cool."

He made a slow circuit around it, inspecting the corners, asking about the wood and some of the finer points of design and construction, repeating the compliment as he ran his hand along the beveled edge of the lid: "Really, really cool."

Then came the wisecracks, and then, with a narrowed gaze, the question. "How deep is it?"

We measured. Twenty-four and a quarter inches.

"Ooh, boy. It's gotta be twenty-two. Maybe twenty-two and a quarter."

He wasn't joking.

The one thing my dad and I had known all along was that we could do whatever we wanted as long as the outside dimensions of the box were smaller than the inside dimensions of a standard burial vault. We'd been careful to take into account the additional width of the handles. Sure, it had grown slightly deeper with Dad's canny addition along the bottom edge, a lip offering a finger hold in case a pallbearer lost his grip on the handle.

But this final process of making the lid had found its own muse, as Dad mulled it over in bed at night and we fixated on the intricacies of carpentry. It had grown taller with each improvement, but only by the thickness of an oak board. Or two.

"Let me make a call," Paul said, pulling his smartphone from his jacket pocket. He asked the receptionist at the burial-vault company for the inside dimensions of a standard vault. She put him on hold.

"You know," Paul said to me as he waited, "you could always get the bronze one. They're bigger." He winked. "Twenty-two grand."

I was losing my humor.

"I always thought it looked deep," Dad said.

"It's deep," Paul confirmed. He stepped toward the casket and set the edge of his palm against the side, about two thirds of the way up. "This is about where the box part usually ends. Then the lid is curved."

We'd been so careful to make sure the box was wide enough to accommodate the span of my bent elbows, but we'd given little thought to its depth. And it occurred to me then that the reason this had not registered was that I'd never climbed inside it. If I'd done so, I probably would have realized just how deep down in the container I lay. On my back, I am not even a foot high. But really—who thinks about these things?

I'd recently learned that John Donne, the English poet, priest, and semi-weirdo, slept in his own coffin in an attempt to embrace and contextualize his mortality. I'd found myself moving through something like a no-man's-land, with this coffin as a seemingly brazen, outward confrontation with mortality, even as I harbored a private internal resistance to that confrontation. It was nearly finished, yet I still couldn't imagine my place inside it.

Paul's call continued. He nodded, listening, then gestured to me to write some numbers down. "Thirty wide, yeah. Eighty long. And twenty-two and a quarter deep. Hmmm. What about a steel vault?"

They chatted a moment more, then ended the call.

"She's going to get some more information and call me back," Paul said.

Turning back to the casket, he explained that our problem was compounded by the fact that our version was rectangular, with a flat top, while commercial caskets have curved tops. So the vaults are arched, meaning the low end of the arch is even lower than the twenty-two-and-a-quarter-inch peak.

Paul looked at the lid. "I wonder if you could set it upside down, with the high part facing in."

Dad grimaced. Paul continued to stare at the box. "You know what else?" He placed his hand on the top edge. "You could cut it down."

I was feeling weak in the knees. The idea of taking a saw to this thing made me queasy. But I was already thinking about the practical reality: the chances of running a saw cut all the way around and having it meet back up with its starting point were nil. I already knew we had some inequalities in the dimensions. Making such a radical adjustment now was a recipe for disaster.

"Or," Paul said, "you could always be cremated." He grinned, but not in his joking manner. This was something closer to sales-manship.

"Gina would never go for that," I said. An avid watcher of *Forensic Files,* she has a distinct fixation on the possibility that one day my body may need to be exhumed. Plus, it would prove that I was wrong about all this.

His phone chirped. He answered. "Hey, Bob." It was the owner. Paul listened and nodded, asking questions, giving the measurements again, shaking his head, asking more questions. Finally, he turned on the speakerphone.

The disembodied voice of Bob informed us that the box we'd built would fit inside a "composition vault," which is slightly larger than a basic concrete vault.

"Does it cost more?" I asked.

"Two hundred dollars more—it's thirteen hundred and ninety-five dollars," Paul said.

I looked at my dad. "So we made a two-hundred-dollar mistake."

"Basically, yeah."

Paul turned off the speaker, bantered with Bob, thanked him, and hung up.

"So," I asked, "let's say I live another forty years. How do we know these dimensions will still be standard?"

"This is a conservative industry. We don't change," Paul said.

Not for the first time, I took selfish comfort in the fact that whatever was wrong with this casket will not be my problem in the moment when it really matters. If the box doesn't fit in the vault, if the lid has warped, if the bottom falls out, I will be in no condition to deal with it. For some reason, in these musings, I always assume Gina will be the one managing the arrangements, and I feel a complicated mix of comfort—there's no one I'd trust more—but also an awareness of the irony that it was our mutual ongoing dispute that led to this coffin in the first place, and that she'd be dealing with its ultimate consequence. In a way, I could say I'd won.

26: WAREHOUSE

Dad and I set off the next morning for Amish country, looking for handles. Paul had assured us that if we dropped in at the small woodworking factory that supplied his funeral home with most of its caskets, the owner—a man who went by the name of Junior Yoder—would probably furnish us with a pair of handles for the sides. "Just tell him I sent you," Paul had said.

I'd ordered all the casket hardware way back at the beginning of the process, including the brackets for the side handles. The cardboard delivery box from the woodworking mail-order company had sat on the floor of Dad's workshop, flaps open, with many of the pieces still in their individual plastic packaging, the box filling with dust throughout the process. Now, resting in the console between the two front seats of my dad's SUV, was one of the hinged brackets. We hoped to obtain a pair of long wooden rails that would fit in its opening.

Ohio is home to nearly seventy thousand Amish people, the largest concentration in the United States. Most live in rural Holmes County, about an hour south of Akron, an area my dad and I had visited together many times. We knew our way around fairly well, and we also knew not to be surprised when we found ourselves lost, following a road that we thought was the right road, even as it led us to a dead end. Faced with the conundrum of which way to turn, we collaboratively decided that left felt most correct, and by "collaboratively," I mean I suggested going right and Dad was sure we should go left. We did. Soon, passing whitewashed houses, clotheslines flapping with blue shirts and trousers, and farm fields being plowed by teams of horses, we found our way to the little town of Dundee. We ate lunch in a general store, then headed up the road to the Behalt Casket Company. Like almost every authentic commercial venture I'd ever encountered in Amish country, this cluster of buildings was neat and unadorned.

We parked—the only car in the lot—and entered through the front door. The big office was sparse and entirely undecorated, but it was fronted by a long, substantial front desk and counter paneled in rich-looking wood. A woman sitting behind it, dressed in an apron and white bonnet, was talking on the telephone. She smiled and held up a finger, signaling us to wait. Dad rested his hand on the counter, admiring it.

The woman finished her call and turned her attention to us. "Well, hello. How can I help you?"

"We're here to see Junior Yoder," I said. "We're friends of Paul Hummel."

"Oh," she said. "Junior's off today."

I explained what we'd come for, and she got back on her phone and asked someone named Miriam to come down to see us.

"This is beautiful work," my dad said, sliding his hand across the counter. "Quarter-sawn oak?"

"Yes," the woman replied. "All quarter-sawn oak. Made right here."

Soon a young woman, also in an apron and head cap, appeared

in the doorway at the end of the counter. "Hello," she said quietly. "I'm Miriam. Junior's not here today. How can I help you?"

"Well," I said, "we're building a casket. And we're hoping to find a set of handles, six feet, that will fit this." I offered her the bracket.

She looked at it, turning it over slowly in her hands, inspecting the opening. "Oh. Well. We don't usually . . . " She looked to the woman at the counter.

"Maybe someone upstairs would know?" the woman said.

Miriam nodded and went back through the door. Beyond its opening, I could see the beginning of a warehouse, shelves stacked with caskets. I turned to the woman. "Do you think we could look around while we're waiting?"

"Oh, sure," she said. "Help yourself."

My father and I passed through the doorway and entered a vast warehouse. We were the only ones present. It was quiet and dimly lit. An open garage bay at the far end offered a distant view of the overcast spring sky. The shelves I'd seen were stacked with steel caskets, wrapped in clear plastic with labels on the ends. To our left were long, deep rows, like library shelves, of wooden caskets stored on their ends, countless dozens, one after another after another.

We drifted toward them and entered one of the rows, moving through the shadowy corridor, deeper and deeper, marveling at the variations and the workmanship, the glossy finishes, the rich tones of wood—brown, red, blond.

"How do they do a curve like this?" my dad said, running his hand admiringly across the lid of one of the upended boxes.

"I don't know," I said. "How do they do any of this?"

We completed one row and entered another. This was the first time I'd seen caskets outside the funeral process—the choosing, the viewing, the service, the cemetery. We were experiencing them as products in a warehouse, in storage, waiting to be ordered and shipped, as though they were mass-produced filing cabinets or truck bumpers. And yet despite the emotionally neutral setting, they exuded an unexpectedly deep tone of humanity. First, in their craft. I don't know how much automation was part of their manufacturing process, but there was an immediate sense of quality and detail that can be attributed only to careful handwork. Dad and I had been working on a single box for some three years, off and on, and I knew how much labor and intricacy had been involved. Each one of these had been built by someone. Each had been designed, joined, sanded, buffed.

More so, however, was the sense of what they would become, the fact that each of these—and there were more than I could count—would be, for a brief yet intense period, the focal point of some family's grief, and that the casket itself was not such a throwaway thing. Each of these would be chosen individually and would provide a vessel—maybe for comfort, maybe for pain, probably for both.

Down one of the rows, we came across a small coffin, proportioned and finished like the others, but unmistakably for a baby. My father and I looked at it for a long moment.

In another opening, we encountered a box laid down in position on a rolling cart.

This one was different—handsome but more rustic. It was a basic rectangle with a flat top and a matte finish. Instead of being a hinged lid, the top was a joined plank affixed with wooden pegs.

"I like this one," my father said, his eyes brightening. "This is *really* neat. This is what I want to be buried in."

He bent down and started working one of the pegs loose. The cart began to roll and I quickly stepped in front of it, stopping it with my palms before it crashed into the domino row of caskets stacked just beyond. Undaunted, Dad removed the pegs and pulled up the lid to peek inside. It was bare, not all frilly and puffy like the usual commercial casket. Just a simple box, yet with the same attitude of craft and attention as the others.

I heard footsteps approaching the stairs above us.

"Ooh." Dad fumbled to get the lid back into place and started working the pegs back in, but he didn't have it on right, and he hurriedly tried to jar it into place. "Help!" he hissed through a half-grin/half-grimace.

I leaned down and worked one corner while he worked another. His ball cap fell off his head, tumbling across the lid and onto the floor. The lid slipped back into place. I grabbed the cap and tossed it to him. He mashed it onto his head, adjusted it, and we exited the row of caskets just as Miriam was coming off the staircase, carrying a long pair of oval-shaped unfinished red oak rods.

"These are the ones we use on most of our caskets," she said. "They look like they'll fit in your bracket."

We followed her back into the office area. I tried the bracket on one of the bars, and it fit just fine. Miriam conferred with the woman behind the counter, who said we could buy the pair for forty dollars. This was far less than the price my dad had gotten previously from a local lumberyard.

I thanked them and paid, and off we went, back up the broken road, past the long furrowed fields and the "Eggs for Sale" signs, to the highway and home.

27: EVERYTHING LINGERS

I thought the death of my mother, and the death of my friend, and the death in some ways of my youth, would teach me something. In fact, I expected it. I believe in the ability of the mind to order things. I believe in it the way some people believe in ghosts.

What seems truest to me now is that death is a shattering. Grief is the chaos of wreckage. Only life can find the pattern, and only in its own sweet time. What I remember from the long season of loss was wanting each day to pass as quickly as possible. To get beyond it. I guess I missed the fact that the by-product of this wish was for my own life to rush by. I don't think I'll ever be beyond it. It just becomes part of the pattern.

As I thought about the long process of working on the casket, which was now a coat of finish away from being done, I returned to the memory of the long summer afternoon I'd spent alone in my dad's barn. John had been gone for a month, my mom had been gone for a year, my shoulder hurt from the sanding, and my mind roamed free.

Life is short.

That phrase had kept recurring, always in John's voice, always in the way he'd said it that night he'd told me we were going to New York together.

I'd resisted it because it was so trite and obvious and seemed to offer no new insight. It was the kind of statement he and I would have rejected, expecting something better. But it kept coming back. And deep into that afternoon in the barn, as "Life is short" played and replayed—a mantra—it began to spawn its own hard truth. Mainly that death wasn't interested in teaching me anything. It could only unlock what was already inside. That time is not for wasting, but restlessness does not enhance it. That old friends make best friends. That wisdom is nothing more than a lifetime of mistakes made. That the longer we live, the less certain we are of anything, especially our own selves. That staring into the silence, thinking a voice will speak back to me, is really just an exercise in staring into the silence. And that depriving myself of certain songs because they hurt too much doesn't make them hurt less.

A long spell of not listening to Radiohead, the Clash, certain Wilco albums, most of Ryan Adams's catalog, and the song "Kung Fu Fighting" (don't ask) as some sort of grief-avoidance strategy was just plain self-depravation. My mother's advice—*Don't become lonely*—helps me understand that sadness is a better companion than it gets credit for. So I started listening again, allowing the questions offered by the songs we'd shared.

Why, I wonder, is my heart full of holes?
Do you realize that everyone you know someday will die?
And you may ask yourself—well, how did I get here?

One of the last things John gave me was the introduction to a new band whose CD sat next to the recliner where he spent the final weeks of his life. Parquet Courts, the group was called.

I hadn't heard of them. But I went out and got the record, and I liked it, in part because they embodied the myth of New York City that John and I had so willingly bought into—a Brooklyn band, clumsy and clever, full of downtown affectation and earnest hyperactivity—but mostly because I admired John's continued passion for discovery even as his breath was failing. He could still teach me things. Parquet Courts would prove, in the short time that followed, to be prolific in a never-not-working sort of way. Under three years following John's death, they released two more full-length albums, an EP, and two additional records under their alter ego, Parkay Quarts. In the song "Berlin Got Blurry" from their 2016 album, *Human Performance*, singer Andrew Savage intones a line that seems delivered straight from John in the sort of communication I still craved from him:

Nothing lasts, but nearly everything lingers in life.

If John remained a constellation of songs and ideas, my mother remained a constellation of artifacts, her presence defined by her countless rosaries and novena candles, by her crossword books and closets full of sweaters and skirts. For a very long time after her death, one year, two years, this was mostly how I reconnected to her—not by spiritual residue but by literal touch, thumbing the green-jeweled golden cross of the St. Patrick's rosary I kept close by in my writing space, pulling down a volume of her OED, looking up words I liked to imagine she had left just for me, using the leftover prayer cards from her funeral as my bookmarks. My dad kept her wedding ring in a little cup in the room where she said her morning prayers, and sometimes

I went in there and slipped it onto my pinkie just to feel it. One day when I was visiting, I spotted the old copy of *Nine Stories* on a bookshelf and asked Dad if I might keep it. He pulled it down and gave it to me.

These things kept her literal. They kept her exact. They kept her from fading. The words and stories in the books would always be the same. The rosary would always have its five decades, each bead hard and round. It was the memories that were more troublesome, the way they slipped around and changed shapes. I got things wrong and out of place. For a long time, I was stuck only on the misery of her final years, her defeated, deflated self, and this became the story of her in my mind. The rest of her essence was somewhere in the corners. Maybe this was a way of protecting myself from the things I missed the most. Maybe it was a way of blaming her for dying. Eventually, though—in great part through those ongoing Sunday-dinner conversations with my father—the rest of her began finding its way back.

"Except for those last couple of years, we had a whole lot of fun," he said one night as we sat with our Manhattans at the kitchen table, drawing out the word "whole" as though filling it up with everything that I'd forgotten belonged there.

In time, missing pieces did work their way back in. I remembered the school lunches she used to pack for me in a brown paper bag with my name on the front in her schoolteacher's cursive, salami and cheese on white bread with yellow mustard, wrapped in waxed paper, and a snack-size bag of taco-flavored Doritos. I remembered a long car trip when she sat in the passenger seat reading *Breakfast at Tiffany's* and came across Holly Golightly's line "Light me a cigarette, darling," the way she lifted her head midsentence to read it aloud with such delicious aplomb that I'm certain, had the car not been moving with such speed and purpose, she would have insisted we stop so she could purchase a pack of Picayunes and try it on for size. I remembered her ravenous laughter as we watched Inspector Clouseau blundering across the evening TV screen, or Steve Martin and Bill Murray in a *Saturday Night Live* skit. I remembered the way she used to mimic David Byrne's hand-chopping motion from Talking Heads' "Once in a Lifetime" video. I remembered the New Year's Day afternoon when I accompanied my parents to the bar where they'd celebrated the previous night so she could retrieve a lost earring, how the owner welcomed them with flowing beard and burly arms and poured me a 7UP with a maraschino cherry for free.

And so, where building my own coffin had at one time seemed like such an enticing metaphor, its assembled form revealed its own truth, the one my father had recognized on the very first day:

It's just a box.

And now it was time to live with it.

One afternoon near the end, as I painted its interior with a coat of pale green paint, I confirmed my previous notion of what to do with it. I would take it home, stand it on end, fit it with shelves, and put it to use. I could keep *Nine Stories* there, and John's Little League team photo, given to me by one of his boyhood friends. I could change its contents as my own life changed. As I drew my brush along the interior corners, I considered the possible locations for this overbuilt, overconceived, highly glorified shelving unit. The living room? No. Gina would never go for that. It could fit in the foyer, but that would mean moving the piano. There was no way it was going to the basement. This would arguably be the nicest piece of furniture in our house. It ought to be seen.

Finally, I arrived at the only viable spot: a foyer on the second floor, against a wall, in a space currently occupied by a very ugly, slightly damaged "wicker" (actually, plastic) bench from Big Lots.

Furniture-wise, this would be a win-win. There was one problem, however. Above that bench hung two very large paintings, one of boxer Michael Dokes and the other of the old Richfield Coliseum, near Cleveland, where the hometown hero once lost a championship bout in a spectacular knockout. Together, they formed a bold and enticing visual narrative, a great rise and fall. But the paintings would have to go.

It's a hard-knock life, John.

As I completed my paint job, I began to work up my overture to Gina. I had continued to dodge her question of where this thing would be stored, and I would need to be persuasive in my delivery. I hoped that she would agree before considering what I, alone in my thoughts, had just realized: if that spot in the hallway indeed became its ultimate (or rather penultimate) resting place, the box would be positioned in such a way that the first thing either of us saw upon departing our bedroom each morning was my open casket.

That same week, I attended a student awards ceremony at the University of Akron art school, in the same building where John had discovered himself, and where his retrospective exhibit had taken place. Two students were being recognized as the Puglia scholarship winners. I sat next to John's parents and his brother in a small, crowded auditorium. A young man and a young woman were called forward, introduced by a faculty member who read a brief description of John's legacy at the university and as a lifelong working artist. They awkwardly made their way from their theater seats to the front of the room and sheepishly received applause. Their faces looked so young.

I wondered what John would think of them. They'd already made the field trip to New York City, several weeks before, during spring break. I wondered what they'd seen, how they saw themselves, how they might have been changed. I wondered if they'd been the same places he'd been, places John would later take me. I wondered who they were becoming.

28: THE MOON FOLLOWS US HOME

The road to my father's house winds through a shady, forested stretch of parkland crossed by bicycle trails and deer paths, adjoined for a spell by a creek that overflows after heavy storms, gouging deep edits of erosion, something of great concern to the township. In the dark, I've seen foxes and skunks skulking along. In the summer, the treetops weave a dense canopy, and the path feels private and close. In the winter, the branches scratch a geometry of loss. When the road opens up to ambling yards and meadows and long stretches of split-rail fence, it rises and falls, and I know where to accelerate to cause that butterfly feeling in my gut. I've known this road all my life. My grandfather lived here when I was a child, and I can remember my father doing the same thing, flying into the dips, making us all quicken with delight, except my mother, who scolded him every time. Leaving there in the twilight, I always marveled at the way the moon followed us home. I still do.

Somewhere along here was a pond deep in the woods. My brothers and cousins and I would troop our way out there sometimes during family gatherings, and in my memory, these were long treks filled with daring and discovery as we encountered piles of Genesee cans and the carcasses of birds and the occasional waterlogged *Penthouse*. We shattered the pond's surface with rocks and bottles and hooked bluegills and concocted fictions of the old man who owned the property and whether we could outrun him and his theoretical dogs. But if I'm right, and I think I am, that pond is the same one I pass by now, just a few yards from the road, cleared of trees, the size of a wading pool, benign as a birdbath.

My father had begun to talk with increasing specificity about moving. The acres of upkeep and the relative distance from the help he might need someday had him devising what he referred to as his "two-year plan": to find an easy-maintenance place in the city, near the part of town where three of his children live. He wanted to downsize his workshop to a basement or garage, to arrange his life into a few rooms, to simplify. He had identified a place that seemed just right, a brick bungalow set back from the street at a quirky angle that made it seem private and alluring. By the manner of his continued investigation, I knew the place had pulled up a chair in his imagination and wouldn't easily leave.

Nothing was imminent, but we'd had enough Sunday-dinner conversations on the subject that driving this route now included the recognition that someday, maybe soon, this road would belong to someone else. As I passed the pond, it began to dawn on me that this was sort of an ending. I was on my way to apply the final coat of varnish, and all that would be left to do after it dried was to haul the coffin out of there and give him back his room. The convertible top was down. I powered up the rise and into the descent, entered the final curve, and turned at the homemade mailbox post into his driveway.

When I walked through the back door calling hello, he was at his little kitchen table, hunched over the order form in one of his woodworker's catalogs. He had announced, not long after our visit to the Amish factory, that he was going to build a casket for himself. He'd been sparked by the simplicity of the pine box with its pegged-down flat lid, and it had wormed into his mind. He'd been lying awake at night working the mental puzzle of dove-tailed corners, and now he sat with his pen and the folded-open catalog, ordering a jig to guide the pattern, a specialized router bit, hinges, handle hardware, and latches.

"We made all the mistakes on yours," he'd told me not long before. "Now I can make mine the right way."

I used to think life was best when I was only vaguely aware of the mistakes I was making, powered by the precarious con-fidence of a young man not knowing how much he does not know. If not for that, I'd never have played guitar in public, nor attempted a novel, nor moved into a condemned house, nor entered the terror of fatherhood. My existence in the dark allowed me experiences I had no other legitimate right to. Fum-bling, blind, and reckless, we find things, including ourselves. But as life has gone on, I've found greater and greater interest in knowing my mistakes, examining them in the light, trying to understand. They are full of information.

"I was going to go down to Keim Lumber today," my dad said, referring to one of his favorite haunts. "But then I remembered something. Let's go out to the barn. I want to show you."

We walked across the backyard together. It was late summer, nearly a hundred degrees, the air so muggy it was hard to breathe. The fluorescent tubes in the barn's exposed ceiling fixtures got temperamental in this kind of weather. They had to warm up for a long time, and it was still never guaranteed that all would come on. But Dad had known I'd be coming and, as usual, had gone out early to flip the switch and give the lights a head start.

We entered. The barn air was cooler. We made our way through the outer room that led to the workshop, past the clutter of dusty broken furniture awaiting his attention, past the battered green lawn tractor and the buckets of garden tools and a pair of his old boots. He led me to a flapped-open cardboard box near the workshop door. Inside was a jumble of wood, dark-stained scraps in various sizes, none over eighteen inches long.

"This was my dad's," he said. "I've had it forever. Black walnut. It was the wainscoting in the old Ohio Edison building downtown. He salvaged it when he worked there."

Like a lot of things in Ohio, the black walnut tree is both common and fine, with inherent difficulties—its green pool-ball-size nuts pummel roofs and break open to a greasy black mess—but with a heartwood as good as any.

The pieces in the box were dusty and ragged with cobwebs strung with rough sawdust. I pulled one out, a plank about twelve inches long, and wiped its surface clean. Like the rest, it was a half-inch thick, smooth, with a coffee-bean tone, beveled at the edges where it once was fitted to another piece. The grain was tight. I could feel its density just by the way it weighed in my hand. Quality, in wood, is straightforward.

Once milled, wood is very close to music, in the way each crafts nature into order, the way each relies on pattern and variation. Both hold internal resonance, endlessly, elusively familiar. On the drive out here, I'd been listening to Ryan Adams's album *Heartbreaker,* an old favorite of John's, and I'd cranked the volume when "Shakedown on 9th Street" came on. Its hard Bo Diddley shuffle and ballsy rasp sounded just like this piece of walnut felt.

I knew this box. It had been in a crawl space in the basement of our old family home, stored in the void between the foundation walls of the addition my dad had built. It was one of a half dozen or so such containers that I've known for as long as I can remember, filled with treasured scraps of wood jumbled up with less notable odds and ends. I have a similar collection at home in the shadows of my own workshop, buckets and boxes, and I know the history of every piece. I still have a few sheets of the green-painted plywood I hauled home to build my ill-fated basement room some forty years ago. And I was sure I remembered this black walnut from my grandfather's workshop, a place from which a number of my dad's tools and my own had come, tangible artifacts that keep his old shop from drifting into fable or, worse, the place beyond memory. When my uncle Jim died, my aunt gave Dad another box of the same wood. He'd thought of the stash as he was sketching inlays for his casket, and when he'd sorted through, he'd realized that between his and his brother's share, he'd have just enough pieces for that purpose.

The box of National Lumber Manufacturers Association wood samples that I inherited from my grandfather includes a rectangular block of black walnut, No. 46, *Juglans nigra*. "USES: Home and office furniture, interior finish and paneling, radios, musical instruments, commercial fixtures, gun stocks, auto trim, steering wheels, caskets, sewing machines, flooring, airplane propellers, clocks, etc."

It had been waiting a long time for this.

He left. He had work of his own to do. Alone in the barn, I entered his workshop through the dirty glass door. It was quiet. The exhaust fan hummed, and I could hear the ebb and flow of the highway traffic beyond the rear wall. Once again, it felt strange to be here without him, yet surrounded by him.

At eighty-four, he repays the blessing of his good health by not wasting any of his days. His life is both small and large, and sometimes it's hard to tell the difference. He has his rhythms, his way of doing things, a new structure since my mom died, but within very old patterns. Just beyond the rear wall of the barn is a corner post on the high stockade fence where, every winter for years, he has mounted a tall plastic Christmas candle, which stays lighted all season, visible from the highway. The year before, a newspaper columnist noticed it, tracked him down, and wrote about his tradition. The article was accompanied by a photograph of Dad posed beneath the candle, a juxtaposition that created the unfortunate illusion that my father has a plastic Christmas candle growing out of the top of his head.

A slew of responses followed from others who'd seen the candle and been similarly charmed by it. One woman thanked him in the newspaper's online comments section, said it made her smile every day as she passed it on her early-morning commute to Cleveland. A stranger mailed him a letter of thanks. Someone delivered him cookies. We called him a celebrity. He liked the attention, though he never expected it. The reason he still puts the candle up is because my mom always insisted on it. Just because she's not sitting across the kitchen table doesn't mean her wishes are gone. It's a good lesson. It's why I can still share a laugh with her.

I pulled my used varnish rag from the end of a sawhorse where I'd hung it wet two days before. It was hardened and held its shape. I could smell its crude caramel as I dropped it with a thunk into the aluminum trash bucket pushed underneath the elevated casket. Warming to the day's work, I took a slow walk around the perimeter of the long box on its sawhorse legs, inspecting the new depth that the finish had brought to the grain, the way it distinguished the oak from the pine.

I decided to climb inside. I knew it was something I was bound to do, and I'd been biding time till what seemed like a meaningful moment, but had resisted for the same reason: it seemed like an overly conceptual ceremony, like that thing where you're supposed to find transcendence by synching up Pink Floyd's *Dark Side of the Moon* with *The Wizard of Oz*.

But now I was here, I was alone, and I was aware that there wouldn't be many more opportunities here in my father's workshop, the place where the box would be its most real. And I had grown to doubt the promise of epiphany. I reached for a short wooden stepstool, set it in place, climbed up, reached one leg over the edge, and stepped in. My boot made a dirty print on the mint-colored paint of the bottom. I brought the other in more carefully. I lowered myself, scooted into position, and reclined.

Paul was right. I felt much deeper inside it than I'd imagined, and there was considerably more length beyond my head and feet than was necessary. Like a child in a parent's overcoat. The lights were bright, and the wood felt hard and cold. I closed my eyes and crossed my arms. The few times I've attempted meditation, I've felt like this, restless and deflective, my consciousness running like a cheap moped. It was important to put things in order. It was important not to forget.

I'd been writing down a set of instructions for how the final pieces would need to go together someday, how the lid and handles would need to be attached, which pieces of hardware went where, and so forth. Gina had wanted me to upholster the interior, but I'd insisted that a quilt and a pillow would be enough. As always, I imagined that the final preparations would be hers, that she would be there at the end. This process had prompted me to do something I'd always wanted to do—to compile my funeral playlist, just as I had done for John's and my mother's memorial services. What I'd found as I'd added and revised was that the list directed itself toward a true north of songs that belonged uniquely and mutually to Gina and me: "Kiss Me on the Bus" by the Replacements, which we'd sung together at the top of our lungs as we drove through the night to our honeymoon . . . "We're Going to Be Friends" by the White Stripes, which we'd played together for our kids every year on the last summer night before school began . . . Bob Dylan's "You're Gonna Make Me Lonesome When You Go," even though I know Dylan grates on her, but that's kind of the point.

This had begun as a conversation with her, one that continued with my father, and now it had found its place in a conversation that has no beginning and no end.

Lying there, I felt my own smallness. It felt all right to me.

AFTERWORD

My father's eighty-sixth year, which would prove to be his last, began at the Washington Square Hotel in Greenwich Village, greeted by the same doorman who'd been John's friend, the one with the quick eyes and the easy humor and the bottle of homemade hot sauce. Dad and I sidled up to the reception counter, a conspiratorial air between us, checking in. We'd secreted my son, Evan, off to wait in Washington Square Park so the hotel staff wouldn't pick up on the fact that we were sneaking three grown men into a room with two twin beds. Spring break. Ohio boys in the big city.

Stealthily reconvened in the little room, I pulled the comforter off my bed and spread it on the floor, grabbed the extra pillow and blanket from the closet, and presented them to Evan. Twenty-one years old, he'd be the one sleeping in the side-nest. Fatherhood has its privileges, even if only the mild upgrade to a cramped twin bed with no comforter.

We set off. Dad had a list. A beer (two, actually) at McSorley's Old Ale House. Spaghetti at Puglia Restaurant in Little Italy. Mass at St. Patrick's Cathedral. A visit to my publisher. At every restaurant and bar, I strategically mentioned that it was my dad's eighty-fifth birthday, even though this was technically true for only one of the four days we spent in the city. I did this not so much to celebrate my father as to try to score free drinks. All it got us was a single limoncello, for him, at his birthday dinner.

This book was finished, but in March of 2017 it was still nine months from publication. My dad had more than a little ambivalence about its contents. All through our process, he'd been asking, *When do I get to read it?*

Just wait, I'd say. *Wait till I think I've got it right.*

Finally, with a near-finished draft, I printed a copy, put it in a three-ring binder, and gave it to him to read. A few days later, he arrived for Sunday dinner, handed the binder back to me and flatly declared, "Well, all my worst fears are confirmed." That was it. My heart sank. I asked him if he wanted to talk about it. He didn't. I tried to assuage his apprehension by assuring him that I don't have enough readers to qualify for a privacy violation. He smiled. Shook his head with that elfish grin and asked me to make him a Manhattan. He neither wanted nor needed to say more. Once again, I'd have to figure him out. He was a private man who liked attention. That may sound paradoxical, but isn't that who my father was? Isn't that what all fathers are? Paradoxes. Singular enigmas to whom their little world comes, wanting, again and again.

The three of us arrived on a weekday morning at the Simon & Schuster building, checked in at security, and headed up in the elevator to Scribner's offices.

"Now, *there's* a bunch of Giffels," Nan Graham, the publisher, sprightly and urbane, declared as we entered the inner offices. Even in a brief conversation, I could tell she enjoyed him. I could tell he enjoyed that she enjoyed him. We settled into a small conference room and sat talking with my editor, John Glynn,

AFTERWORD 241

for about an hour. Dad was curious about the process. John, young enough to be his grandson, wanted to hear his stories. He told my dad that he had no woodworking skills of his own, that the only thing he and his dad had ever built together was a beer pong table. People always seemed to want to tell my father about their own deficiency with tools, as though in deference or confession. (Dad mentioned later, not unkindly, that John had mistaken "lacquer" for "varnish.") As we walked together back to the elevator, John promised to send him a box of recent releases.

Our chief destination awaited. The Brooklyn Bridge. This had been on my father's bucket list for years, to walk across, to see and feel the wonder of what David McCullough had described in *The Great Bridge*, one of Dad's favorite books. He had pages of notes in his jacket pocket. He knew all about the engineers and the scandals and the braiding of the steel wires. He knew about the caissons and the bends and the falcons nesting above. It was a brisk, sunny spring morning as we set off among the hundreds of other walkers, stopping along the way to take in the view, pose for pictures, read the brass plaques. At one stretch, I pulled a pen from my bag and added to the graffiti on an I-beam: *Giffels Boys 3-29-17*. We made a long, slow walk of it, taking it all in. When we reached the Brooklyn side, we found a beer joint, ordered a round, and sat and talked for a long time.

Back home, he continued working in his barn on his own casket, tended to his gardens, took his self-prescribed two-mile walks in the park near his house. He planned an expanded family vacation on Lake Michigan—his children and grandchildren, nieces and nephews, all who could make it there. The visit to New

York seemed to have softened my father's apprehension. As the months wore on toward publication, I noticed him mentioning— often to people who hadn't asked—about this book his son had written, about him, and a coffin.

By fall, we knew something was wrong: the sickness he felt, the pain in his side, the things he continued to try to ignore. He was leaving the house less often but still enjoying his life there. He read every one of the books John Glynn had sent him in a big box, told me he broke down crying at the end of *Shoe Dog*. Which was strange, because I'd only seen this man cry once, and it was over a whole lot more than a sneaker mogul.

As Gina and I planned the annual Thanksgiving dinner at our house, a sprawling affair with thirty-odd guests (in the case of my family, just remove the hyphen, as a certain number of the guests are indeed odd), he insisted on cooking the second turkey. As the holiday approached and his condition grew more worrisome, we tried to talk him out of it, but he was adamant. He was cooking the damn turkey. It was already in his freezer, he said. He'd researched the brine. The only concession he'd give was to accept help lifting the heavy plastic bag filled with brine and the bird into and out of his refrigerator. It was more than he could handle. But it was the only thing he couldn't handle.

He was, as always, the first to arrive. He came in through the back door into the steamy, herb-scented kitchen, set the roasting pan on the stovetop, dropped into his regular chair at the kitchen table, and asked for two sticky notes and a marker. On one slip, he wrote, "I'm." On the other, "Fine." He stuck them to his chest, his cheeky way of forestalling the inevitable questions from family who'd only been getting the news via group texts and emails.

"I'm fine."

In the long view, he was. At one of his last Sunday dinners, he allowed that he knew where this was headed, and that he was at peace with it. "The only thing that makes me sad," he said that night, "is that I know other people will be sad."

The original hardcover edition of this book was released on January 2, 2018.

Three days later, he died, at peace, in hospice, with all of us there.

The last book he read was this one.

The last thing he finished in his workshop was his own casket.

The last thing he wrote was a poem, in bright green ink on a sheet of his engineer's grid paper, left on his desk in an envelope printed with the instructions that it be opened at his funeral.

I'm like an oak tree in autumn:

The oak leaves die and fall to the ground
Just as my body dies and returns to the earth

But the oak is still alive and looking forward to spring
And so my soul remains alive
Anticipating the eternal spring!

—May 2018

APPENDIX:
FUNERAL PLAYLIST TOP 20

1. "Streets of Laredo," Tex Ritter
2. "This Must Be the Place," Talking Heads
3. "If I Should Fall from Grace with God," the Pogues
4. "New Day Rising," Hüsker Dü
5. "I'm in Love with a Girl," Big Star
6. "Kiss Me on the Bus," the Replacements
7. "Moon River," Audrey Hepburn
8. "Do You Realize??," Flaming Lips
9. "Beautiful Boy," John Lennon
10. "Can't Help Falling in Love," Elvis Presley
11. "We're Going to Be Friends," the White Stripes
12. "The Jackson Song," Patti Smith
13. "Jesus, Etc.," Wilco
14. "1952 Vincent Black Lightning," Richard Thompson
15. "We Will Become Silhouettes," the Postal Service
16. "You're Gonna Make Me Lonesome When You Go," Bob Dylan
17. "Time," Tom Waits
18. "If You See Her, Say Hello," Jeff Buckley (*Live at Sin-é* version)
19. "Monkey Gone to Heaven," the Pixies
20. "It's a Beautiful Day," Pizzicato Five

ACKNOWLEDGMENTS

My biggest, loudest, sloppiest thanks go to my main man, Thomas E. Giffels, for his patience and unfailing humor as he rolled with all of this and weirdly made it make sense.

As always, I owe gratitude beyond calculation to my agent, Daniel Greenberg, and to all the good people in the fur-lined vaults of Levine Greenberg Rostan Literary Agency.

I knew I was in good hands with John Glynn as an editor when he took one look and said this isn't really a book about a coffin. He was right, and he guided with a careful hand and a big heart and made me feel good about everything even when it was hard.

Thanks as well to the entire Scribner family, especially Susan Moldow, Nan Graham, Roz Lippel, Colin Harrison, Sarah Goldberg, and Rosie Mahorter. A special shout-out to Lauren Lavelle, who has moved on in pursuit of her own dreams but not before helping me above and beyond with mine.

This book project began as a wee-hours conversation with Brant Rumble, who challenged and championed it and brought it into being, and who will always be a friend, no matter where he is.

Bob Ethington, the Max Perkins of Akron, is as generous a

first reader as anyone could hope for. Yet again, I'm thankful for his trenchant insight and his tequila brotherhood.

The following people read versions of this manuscript and told me exactly what they thought. I thank them nonetheless: Andrew Borowiec, Chris Drabick, Gina Giffels, Chris Horne, Amy Keating, Chuck Klosterman, Eric Morris, Dave Rich, and Eric Wasserman. Dave Lucas provided crucial feedback and guidance, not to mention a rare and treasured friendship. I'm sorry I drank all your Jameson. But not really.

Many thanks to the editors who have offered opportunity and guidance (and money gigs) along the way, most notably: Yoni Appelbaum, David A. Graham, and Rebecca J. Rosen at *The Atlantic*, Anne Trubek and Martha Bayne at Belt Publishing, Steve Gleydura at *Cleveland Magazine*, Dan Fierman at *Grantland*, Melanie Anagnos at Lumina, John Glassie at *The New York Times Magazine*, Eric Nuzum at WKSU, and all my former colleagues at the *Akron Beacon Journal*. Hallelujah in memoriam to Joan Rice, the calm in every storm.

Speaking of which, a substantial portion of Chapter 17, "Turning Fifty," appeared originally on Grantland.com. Part of Chapter 23, "The Coffin Problem," was adapted from an essay published as "The White Bedroom" in the journal *Lumina*. The book's afterword appeared in slightly different form on the Atlantic.com.

I am profoundly indebted to the Puglia family, especially John's sons, Jonathan and Sam—both now living in New York City—his parents, Gino and Carol, his brother, Anthony, and Anthony's wife, Jennifer, and his sister, Sue, and her husband, Bill, for sharing John with me and trusting me with his story.

I am privileged to spend my days with interesting people,

talking about books and writing. Thanks to all my students, colleagues, and friends in the University of Akron English Department and the Northeast Ohio Master of Fine Arts program in creative writing, especially Robert Pope, Mary Biddinger, and Eric Wasserman.

As I am defined in every way by my life with Gina Giffels, I'll thank her here on this page because I can, and then again tomorrow over coffee, and the next day and the next day, forever, unless I sleep in.

Finally, I'm deeply grateful to the University of Akron Faculty Research Fellowship and the Ohio Arts Council for generous support during the writing of this book.

ABOUT THE AUTHOR

David Giffels is the author of *The Hard Way on Purpose: Essays and Dispatches from the Rust Belt*, nominated for the PEN/Diamonstein-Spielvogel Award for the Art of the Essay, and the memoir *All the Way Home*, winner of the Ohioana Book Award. His writing has appeared in the *New York Times Magazine*, the Atlantic.com, *Parade*, the *Wall Street Journal*, Esquire.com, *Redbook*, and many other publications. He also was a writer for the MTV series *Beavis and Butt-Head*. He is an associate professor of English at the University of Akron, where he teaches creative nonfiction in the Northeast Ohio Master of Fine Arts Program.